Basingstoke To Benidorm

First paperback edition (Amazon)
October 2024

Cover design by Craig Killick

ISBN 9798342025546
(paperback edition)

Pre Introduction
Introduction

Please excuse my indulgence in writing this book. I wanted to document the journey of my life, and I love writing, so why not? I thought.

Any profits, probably in pence rather than pounds, will end up with The Pink Place Charity. So, once again, why not?

Although the book has nothing to do with the charity - that's a disclaimer as there might just be some fruity language - if this book can help them in any way, I am glad to help.

The team, helped by a fantastic group of volunteers, do a great job of supporting people with Cancer, offering group well-being sessions, counselling, complementary therapies and other support services at a time when they face one of the biggest battles of their life.

This book was written and proofread by me and a select few as I can't afford editors, sub-editors, and possibly sub-sub-editors.

So, please exuse any typos, theey r not intensional.

PS. If you do see any typos, be a love and email me: ck@craigkillick.co.uk
PPS. If you fancy donating any extra pounds to The Pink Place Cancer Charity, please go to their website: thepinkplace.org.uk

Basingstoke to Benidorm

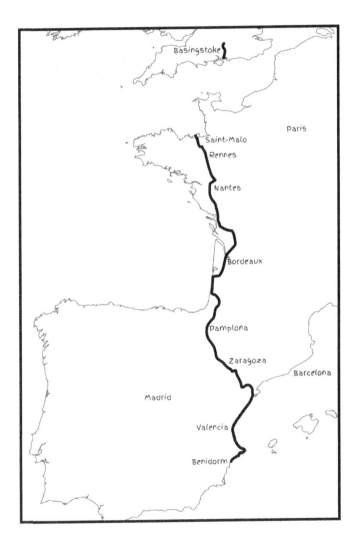

Contents

Introduction

Life's a funny fucker. If you believed everyone around you as they tell you the filtered version of their lives, or, took for gospel the films you waste time watching, with one eye on your phone, you'd look at yourself as an adult and always feel like you're falling short.

In 2017, I got divorced. All my future plans and goals were kicked firmly into touch and had to be realigned with my new life. On one hand, it was terrifying. I pictured myself as an old man sitting all alone in a bedsit. On the other hand, combined with crossing my fifty-year birthday line, it has been absolutely liberating.

Ian, a good friend, cheered me up over a casual office chat one morning just as I hit the big Five-O in April 2021 by announcing that I was now in Sniper's Alley - anything could take me out at any time. To be fair, seeing as my dad and both grandfathers died early from heart issues, I'm actually amazed I've made it this far, especially when I look in the mirror and see a chubby grey buffoon staring back at me.

It's why, at the age of 53, I found myself ready to embark on a solo cycle ride from Basingstoke to Benidorm, attempting to travel over 1,800km under my own steam over three weeks. Just me, a bike called Terence, and the overwhelming need for a bit of adventure.

I first planned to do this cycle ride in 2019. It was firmly in the diary; I even had the ferry booked. But I had to postpone it because of work pressures at the time. Then, a year later, COVID came along, decimating my beauty business. This unhappy accident relieved me of the very same work pressures I'd been having and a lot of stress besides. Every cloud and all that.

So here I was, four years later, a stone and a half heavier and nervously excited, like a small child before a birthday. Because - and this is the reality - if I keep putting this cycle ride off, time, quite literally, may well run out on me.

We're good at that, aren't we? Putting stuff off and focusing on all the wrong things in life until it's too late, then wishing we'd done things differently, full of regrets. My generation is blessed with so much luxury that we think that time, literally, won't catch up with us. Good luck with that.

But, if there is one crucial thing I've learned over the past seven years, guided by the wayward lead of my amazing new partner, Lorraine - sometimes, you've just got to 'do shit now'.

So, way out of my comfort zone and finding inspiration and drive from books, documentaries and social media feeds of the many people who have had adventures like this before me, I'm ready: Ready to challenge myself, ready to meet some interesting new people, and ready to have one of the most amazing experiences of my life.

Some may call it a mid-life crisis.
Me; I call it a mid-life awakening.

My Cycling Career

I've been cycling as an adult since my early thirties. As a kid, I was never off my bike, whether it was a Budgie, a Grifter, or a racer with the handlebars turned upside down doing jumps down the school playground, usually over some small children lying down, side-by-side in a row, absolutely full of fear. It was liberating in a world where parents didn't check on you every ten minutes or have some secret tracking device on your mobile phone.

As young as twelve, we'd often cycle our bikes into the town of Basingstoke, then across Eastrop Park, venturing out to the countryside village of Old Basing to play in the river and light fires. It felt like miles and miles and miles. It was less than four.

Then, in my teens, I persuaded my parents to let me buy the most awesome bike in the world - a Raleigh Team Banana racing bike. It stood out so vividly on the racer bike page of my mum's catalogue and was my biggest crush up to that point in my life - well, after a couple of girls in my tutor group.

By then, I had a paper round earning the princely sum of £3.80 a week. I could use my wages and pay for the bike weekly from the catalogue. These were the days when you were encouraged to buy something now and pay it off over a year or so. Some things never change - it was like the Klarna of the 1980s.

Many happy days were spent with that Littlewoods catalogue, especially leading up to Christmas. I'd thumb through the toy section with my brother, both of us taking turns to choose what we'd like from each page, only to get none of it from Santa on the big day. Or, if I was alone, I'd stare in wonder at the lady's underwear section, trying to fathom out why my body felt a little bit funny down below. Ah, such innocence.

Being the conservative type, my dad was more challenging to persuade than my mum when it came to me buying a bike 'on tick'. He argued that by the time I'd paid for it at £2.50 a week for 50 weeks, I'd be bored of it. His more sensible proposal was to save the money first and see if I still wanted it in 50 weeks time. My argued response to that was, 'But Dad, you just don't understand! It's not fair!'.

After much discussion (moodiness and nagging), he finally gave in, and my beautiful yellow and black road bike arrived. I loved it, and rode it around with pride - for a couple of months. He was, of course, absolutely right.

I rode bikes up until the age of 19 when I passed my driving test. I still vividly remember cycling the four miles and back to my job at Tesco Chineham as a 16-year-old, complete with a CD Walkman hung around my neck, listening to Simple Minds. Every time you hit a bump on the path, the track would jump. There were many bumps. But Hey, Hey, Hey, Hey.

But, it was no way to get a girlfriend, riding on two wheels; four wheels and petrol engines beckoned. My cycling days were over. That said, it turns out you need something called a 'personality' to attract women above and beyond a Mint Green VW Golf Mark II.

At the age of 32, I found myself running a design agency with my friend Rob. We'd got involved working for the charity Make-A-Wish Foundation UK. At the time, they organised an annual charity cycle ride from Camberley to Portsmouth, and before I knew it, I had bought a bike and signed up. 52 miles. This led to another ride, which meant I had to buy a new bike, of course, which led to my first London To Paris in 2005. My second followed a few years later, and I continued riding. It was my way to stave off the growing middle-aged spread. That didn't quite go to plan. I'd discovered red wine and French cheese at the same time as cycling. Comme ci, comme ca.

Moving forward a few years, the topic of cycling from John o'Groats to Land's End kept coming up in pub conversations. My circle of friends had evolved by then. It now included some like-minded cyclists, deluded into thinking we looked athletic in lycra while regularly huffing and puffing our way through a 30-mile ride before having a pint.

And so it was, in the first week of July 2016, I found myself in the worldwide top ten on Strava for distance cycled as we ploughed through an average of 100 miles a day over ten days through Scotland and down to Cornwall via Basingstoke. It was an experience I will never forget, and somewhere, deep down, I have some fantastic memories. I also realise now that we were so intent on doing the distance each day that I didn't really enjoy it very much.

I do have some very specific memories, though. Riding up the Glencoe Pass from Fort William will stay with me forever. I'd been left behind by the small group of lither men I was with, so I was left to cycle at my own pace. The views were so spectacular it was the one time over those ten days that I thought to actually stop and soak it in. The reflection of the sun shimmering off cascading water down the sheer face of the mountains; the road cut into the rocks crawling up the side of the pass, trying to find the path of least resistance. It was the ingenuity of man's construction abilities versus the sheer scale of nature. Spectacular. As for the rest of the ride, I just remember it being a slog.

I learned my lesson, and in May 2017, with some friends (including Ian, trying to stave off a Sniper's bullet or two), I rode up the Tourmalet pass from Luz-Saint-Sauveur in France. Only 19km, but a gruelling average incline of 7% with no respite, all the way to the top. The four of us on the trip had split up after less than 1km in, so I was on my own for the ride. I stopped a couple of times. I marvelled. I wondered why a vulture kept circling me. (He was probably looking down thinking, nah, he ain't gonna make it, I'll keep an eye on him.)

Photos never do views like that justice. Being on a bike and not stuck in a car imprinted some powerful memories that day, which I look back on clearly with pride and wonder to this day. As a result, two and a half hours of cycling hold more joy and memory for me now than ten days traversing an entire country doing JOGLE (John o' Groats to Lands End).

By then, I'd got wrapped up in a little group called Arkriders, which raised a lot of money organising cycle ride challenges over the next four years. Our 2017 ride from Basingstoke to Paris was a highlight for me, and when I mention it to anyone, the first thing I tend to say is, 'I've been on quieter stag weekends'. Once again, enjoying the experience of the ride and the people around me was more important than the ride itself.

But organising people, paperwork, and personalities is tiring, as is the constant moaning. So, the thought of a solo ride was born. Just me, without 40 people questioning things at every turn, sounded bliss. The charity part would come later, but Basingstoke to 'somewhere' became the plan. That somewhere became Benidorm.

As previously mentioned, the ride was all set for Autumn 2019 but had to be canned due to work pressures. But, after that false start and getting back to some sort of normal after the pandemic, in January 2023 I decided the time was right to start planning for 2024. What could go wrong?

Planning and Preparation

Cycling is simple. It's a bit like riding a bike. But, for someone like me, who likes to know details and how things work, it can get very deep, very quickly. I'm not one of those people with numerous bikes in their garage (unless three counts), but when it comes to the machines themselves, I need to know how they work so that I can fix stuff and improve the machine to suit me. I'm no racing snake, so comfort would be paramount, especially if I planned to cycle every day for three weeks. I'd need the right bike to suit me and my challenge, and I'd need to get it as quickly as possible to get used to it. I hit the Internet.

Now, I don't know about you, but researching products online can be a bit of a rabbit hole. I'll find a product and be on the verge of adding it to the basket when one person pops up with a negative comment or review and it confuses the hell out of me. I think I prefer the old days when the only option you had when you were buying a bike was to pootle down to your local cycle shop, where a kindly older gentleman would bumble through describing his selection of just three suitable bikes. But, alas, here I was, in the largest supermarket in the world, full to the brim with expert reviewers. And I use the word expert with so much tongue in cheek, it sounds like expuwt.

After lots of searching, reading, and oh-so-nearly buying bikes, I eventually decided on a dedicated touring bike - the Genesis Tour De Fer. Just to give you a very quick run down, touring bikes are built differently than road or mountain bikes. They have extended frames, usually built from steel, that are more robust to carry the extra weight that touring bikes need to carry - ideal for the luggage I would need and necessary for carrying my paunch.

This bike not only had good reviews, but I also liked the sound of the components, especially the gearing. Without sounding nerdy, having a sound gearing system on a bike is an essential part of cycling effectively. In the past, I've had all sorts of issues with inferior components on bikes, including gears that don't stop jumping, which is not ideal when you are halfway up a steep hill. In my experience, it's money well spent paying for a better setup. So I did.

The day of my bike's arrival came. It was in a huge box, in pieces, and I immediately stopped what I was doing and went about figuring out how to put all the bits together. As annoying as this can be - making your own bike - it's an excellent way to get a grip on how things go together and how the machine works. As someone who has been so used to road bikes over the years, the first thing I noticed was how heavy the bike was. It also had many more bits, including the all-important pannier frames, mudguards, and a set of lights connected to a dynamo built into the hub of the front wheel.

With the bike built, I took a quick ride around the block. I already loved it. It was so much more comfortable than my road bike, especially over the lovely English tarmac assault course we call roads. The upright seating position, along with the size of the bike itself, made it feel a lot safer, too. We were going to get along grand.

Obviously, I had to give the bike a name, and Terence The Tourer was born. Yes, another alliteration and a small homage to Terry Wogan. I sometimes think I should have been too young to be a fan. But I wasn't. Ever. Radio Two was a calling that came early for me. Perhaps it's because I've felt like a 50-year-old since I was 20, with my age growing into me, rather than the other way around.

I used to love the breakfast show on Radio Two, with Wogan's calm manner, his soft Irish accent, and the way he always seemed to be taking the piss, especially out of himself. A kindred spirit, if you will. Albeit I don't have a calm manner or a voice for radio, I'm just very good at taking the piss.

Now, anyone who has ever cycled will know that buying a bike is only the start of the money pit, the first few digs of the spade, if you will. I already had a road bike and all the gear to go with it, but Terence was a different beast. My bank balance was already squeezing its bum cheeks. Further expense was going to follow, and follow fast it did.

A new leather saddle, bags, tools, bottles, and clothes arrived. Then, of course, if I was going to be a proper travelling cyclist, I'd need camping gear - a tent, sleeping bag, mini air bed, and a gas stove. As luck would have it, like most of the nation, I'd already made some obligatory Covid lockdown purchases that might be relevant - stuff I'd used once, before piling it in the garage and never using it again. And no, I'm not talking about the paddle board or the kayak that I still trip over whenever I need to get something out of storage; I'm talking about the camping equipment I'd bought and used for one disastrous trip to Devon.

I rifled through the piles of kit, throwing aside the body boards, wet suits and life jackets bought during the same period. The only thing that ended up being of any use from my extensive 2020 investment into camping equipment ended up being a cheap sleeping bag.

I really must stick all that stuff on Facebook Marketplace one of these days to clear my garage, if nothing else. I imagine 'blokes' coming around to look at my wares for sale, hands in pockets, playing it cool, getting ready to haggle, before having a big sniff, then nonchalantly asking, 'Lockdown purchase, mate?'

My cycle route from Basingstoke to Benidorm was also starting to take shape. I knew I wanted to cycle down to Portsmouth and get through the English leg in one day. No offence to Brits, but they're not the best road companions.

I get it, a lot of cyclists are dicks, with no care for car users. But, as a cyclist, it's pretty unnerving when you have a tonne or two of metal gliding past, less than a metre away from your elbow, with the driver smoking a vape and the music on full blast. If you cycle on larger roads, people hate you. If you opt for country lanes, people tut at you and tailgate. Such fun! In fact, the current state of the roads in England makes me glad I'm no longer on a road bike with a 25mm tyre between me and the tarmac and stones. That extra 9mm width on Terence's tyres makes all the difference when I'm trying to swerve a pothole full of water sufficient enough to moor a small boat, while a Renault Twingo's engine screeches to my right.

Where were we? Ah, yes, the route. Strava, an online sports tracking platform, would be my friend for this part of the planning, helping me to plot my route. I had decided on a 22-day trip with one day of rest, so I would start by planning the complete route before dividing it up. Simple.

I toyed with traversing the Pyrenees, testing myself once again on the Tourmalet, but the dates wouldn't work. I would be there too early in the year, and the mountain passes would still be closed from the winter season. I'd like to say I was disappointed, but I think I was more relieved. I sometimes forget I'm a 53-year-old lump of raw dough and not Chris Froome.

As I plotted the route through France on my computer, I kept an eye on the elevation - the total number of metres I'd have to climb. Distance is one thing on a cycle ride, but elevation makes a huge difference, especially with the weight I'd be carrying.

Put me next to a fellow cyclist of a similar age downhill, and I'd whip them. But as soon as any incline appears, my speed reduces to a crawl, as if someone has just unplugged my battery. It's called Physics, apparently, and my lack of appreciation of its rules (so many rules!) may explain why I got an Ungraded result on my O'Level Physics exam back in 1987. Either that or the fact that I discovered two incredibly significant things at the age of 15. Firstly, I discovered that I could mimic my dad's signature sufficiently for my form tutor not to question it. Secondly, I realised how easy it was to bunk off school. It was a marriage made in heaven and allowed me to enjoy many an afternoon wasting my life, which seemed important at the time.

Having plotted my route down to Southern France, I took a deep breath as I added the Pyrenees crossing on. The elevation of the route so far, already programmed in, suddenly began to flatten as Strava chugged away to include the mountains. It was only to be expected. At least I knew what I would be facing.

Not knowing Spain well, I was adamant that I wanted to go down through the middle of the country with my route. I wanted to see Spain, to arrive at the Spanish version of Basingstoke one night and meet real Spanish people who had just finished their shift at the local El Sainsbury's warehouse, rather than fly down the Costa Brava with all the tourists. So, I clicked on Benidorm as the final destination and let Strava do its magic. I could tweak the route afterwards if need be.

Christ, alive! France became as flat as a pancake. The Pyrenees pass I'd already programmed in began to shrink, as Spain reared its mountainous interior like the birth of The Fortress of Solitude in Superman (the original 1978 movie, if you were wondering).

Yes, Spain was looking a little 'lumpy', to say the least. Lumpy is something that lycra-clad cyclists love popping into conversations when they're talking about a hilly route. 'Yes, that 50k ride was a little lumpy today!'. The fact that they usually have the frame of a prepubescent teenage boy makes me just want to slap them. In fact, I would, except I'm usually too out of breath after riding the lumps!

Having read some great books on bike touring journeys like my own, especially the brilliant Spain to Norway on a Bike Called Reggie by Andrew Sykes, I knew that tourist areas are not a fun place to stay, especially when camping. People tend to have a different agenda from someone focusing on human-powered travel and a good night's sleep, favouring themselves being well-oiled rather than their gears and chains. So, I wanted to avoid the coastal route if possible. Besides, as I honed the route, I discovered towns like Cuenca and Alcalá del Júca inland in Spain, which sure did look pretty on Google images.

Eventually, after weeks of chopping and changing, I decided on a route consisting of 21 days on the bike and a day off in Bordeaux, where my partner Lorraine would fly out to meet me to bring anything I lacked, such as a personality.

Undoubtedly, she would also miss my delightful smile after six days without seeing me.

Some of the planned cycling days were longer than others, and they ranged from 52km to 115km. By being flexible - not one of my strong points - I could take a second day off in Spain if I needed to or take a detour if I so desired. In terms of climbing, the days ranged from the least amount of 148m on the day coming out of Bordeaux to 1,556m towards Molina de Aragón, northeast of Madrid. For comparison, the day crossing over the Pyrenees was less than that at 'only' 1,300m. In the back of my mind, I always had the coastal option to fall back on if I was struggling along the way, so I pinpointed Pamplona as a place to regroup if I needed to.

Another area that needed planning was kit - what to take with me. I was very keen to document the ride, and I love a bit of tech, which means computers and cameras. But obviously, I'd have to carry anything I took on the bike with me. I started looking at socks in terms of grammes and weighing up what was more critical - warm clothing or my drone. Of course, logic went out of the window.

It also meant spending a stupid amount of money on things I didn't really need. (Perhaps I could put them in my garage with the kayak?) Despite researching and looking into what other people had taken on their rides, I couldn't pinpoint what was essential and what was a luxury. In the end, my partner reminded me that they do, in fact, have shops in both France and Spain, and I could buy stuff along the way if I felt I needed to. It sounds rather obvious when you say it out loud. Hopefully, I'd be able to survive the entire three weeks with only my own logic to rely on.

During the entire 15-month planning stage, two key things happened. The first one related to the time of year I was planning to ride, which was organised around a friend's birthday. It would have made much more sense to be doing the ride in the autumn, but I was doing it in the Spring to fit in around his plans. And right up until three months to go, that was the idea. Then he bailed on going, but my flights and ferry were already booked, so I had no choice but to stick with the dates. Luckily, Lorraine and other friends stepped up to help me and meet me with my bike box to bring Terence home. Panic diverted.

I also decided to raise money for a charity. The Pink Place came into my life in April 2023 when my small beauty business donated some products to a fundraising fashion event. After a conversation or two, my arm was twisted (in a nice way) to start helping the charity a bit more, and soon I was headlong into flexing my marketing muscle to help with fundraising as a trustee.

The Pink Place is not a big charity, but it helps a lot of adults in Basingstoke who have had a cancer diagnosis. The NHS supply the treatment, but it's the well-being support they can't provide. That's where The Pink Place comes in. Besides, why not? I'd be doing the ride, come what may, so I thought I might as well tag something worthwhile to it. With any luck and with good support from my network, I could help make a real difference to their bank balance.

Being a trustee of a charity is good fun. I've got to meet and deal with people I would never have met while doing something worthwhile. Besides, while other charities have marketing and fundraising teams, we don't. So, every communication and contact we can make is a bonus, and that's where I can help.

Come the autumn of 2023, Terence and I were out regularly with no baggage attached, and I would go cycling, just to get some distance in. Then, bit by bit, I slowly added bags to get used to the bike with the extra weight and practice balancing with a different weight distribution. I wasn't too worried about long distances; it was just about getting out regularly.

And boy, was I enjoying this new way of cycling. It was so much more relaxed than riding on a road bike. I wasn't trying to get anywhere quickly, and I wasn't looking at my bike computer every few seconds to check my speed, so I could look up and pootle along if I fancied.

I'm lucky as well with where I live; I have some great surroundings. Having cycled in many places across the UK and Europe, Hampshire is a stunning place to ride a bike, with its rolling hills and small villages. I am blessed to have it all on my doorstep.

I found a few documentaries online to watch for inspiration. Home2Home on Netflix was good, and We Are All In This Together on Amazon was also enjoyable. I took notes and got some fresh ideas, especially about charging electrical devices in bathrooms on campsites - that would end up being a useful tip on my travels.

Watching these films, I started to realise something significant. Like so many people, here I was, marvelling at other people having grand adventures in their lives through the safety of a screen, sitting on my couch, eating chocolate and drinking wine. I should be out there doing something - living a little more. As an adult, I've got far too used to spending time inside, whether working or during downtime, enjoying the comfort that goes with it. And, as much as I've always liked the reassuring comfort of home, it can get monotonous.

I'd love to be more active and spend more time outdoors. When I do, I realise how much I love it, untethered from my computer, enjoying nature for what it is in its beautiful simplicity. Was it time I finally made the most of things in later life? Or have I been waiting, like a Leming, for something big to happen to me - a sign, perhaps? This adventure was fast becoming the wake-up call I needed.

My ride from Basingstoke to Benidorm was flicking more and more positive neural switches. I was looking forward to stepping outside of my comfort zone, seeing new places at a pace where I could notice things, and living a little - maybe even living a lot! I imagined sitting in bars, trying to chat with people in Spanish, a language I have been trying to learn on and off for about twenty years. 'Estoy en mi bicicleta desde Inglaterra, Si.' I even wrote down some core phrases in French and Spanish to answer all the questions I may have thrown at me along the way.

As Christmas came and went, and 2024 arrived, the January weather was not ideal, and my cycling was either very cold, very wet, or both. The training was slow, and it was hard to get motivated. But, by March, with a month to go, and despite the weather still being very wet and cold, I was out regularly and comfortable with my fitness level.

I also started having sports massages to ease my stiffening legs. They were enlightening in terms of stretching. My calves, which had been rock-hard for as long as I could remember, started to flex. Pains in my feet began to subside because of something being stretched in my hip and lower back. Suddenly, I didn't have to start rocking myself a couple of times like a discus thrower to get enough momentum to roll out of bed in the morning. I could stand on one leg. I could tie my shoelaces without losing my breath. I was turning into Daley Thompson; I was sure of it. I was feeling great.

But deep inside, the nerves were starting to kick in. I'm not completely sure why. I had planned, trained and prepared, but other people's constant questioning certainly didn't help.

'But who's supporting you? No-one? You must have, though; you can't do that all on your own.'

'Oooo, how will you cope three weeks on your own? You'll get so lonely!'

Will I? I think I'll be okay. Especially not having to answer your daft bloody questions. Besides, I won't be alone; I'll have Terence.

I always find people's assumptions and assertions interesting - how they place their shit on you, whether they really know you or not. People (who don't know me well enough) often say I am a bit miserable. My demeanour probably doesn't help. But the fact is, I'm not. I'm just pragmatic and say things based on how I see them. Like Kipling, I subscribe to the idea that highs and lows are identical imposters dressed up slightly differently.

'You must be super-excited?' Nope.

'You'll feel so down when it's all over!' Wrong again.

Over the years, I've done enough discovery work on myself - religious, philosophical, and psychological - to understand exactly who I am, warts and all. I'm imperfect, 100%. But carrying my own shit around doesn't mean to say I have to accept others who want to rain on my parade. So, when the comments continued, I just started smiling, ignoring everything that was being said.

Social media was also a challenge I needed to face. These days, I subscribe to the unfashionable idea that I don't have to share every emotion online or promote every futile thing I've done to get external approval. That said, I knew I had to re-open old social media accounts to share stuff, especially if I wanted to improve my profile for fundraising. But I was happy to keep that relatively low-key. At the end of the day, the purpose of going social was to raise money, not try to become the next middle-aged influencer 'living their best life!'.

I've used social media for fundraising before. It can be very powerful. It can also be frustrating. Sometimes, with my posts, I just want to rehash the Bob Geldof Live Aid moment and say, 'Fuck the likes and the self-serving comments! Just give us your bloody money!' I didn't though; that would be rude.

My ride is a perfect example of what I mean when it comes to actually doing something versus sitting on the sidelines simply commenting about someone else doing it. I genuinely believe that any person in reasonable health could do a ride like the one I had planned. Yes, it's not easy-peasy-lemon-squeezy, but it is a very doable challenge. You just have to get up off your arse and do it. Plan, prepare, and, ultimately, just keep moving your legs - it's not rocket science. Stop spectating and start participating. Perhaps it's the perception of what it may take being more of a barrier than just doing the thing itself? Whether it's Couch To 5k, a Half Marathon, or cycling to Spain, there are plenty of people who can, and plenty of people who do. It's not a competition.

With today's technology, my cycle ride will be easier than ever before. If I'd cycled across Europe pre-internet, with paper maps and no idea where hotels or campsites might be, it would have been infinitely more challenging. But here I am on a lightweight bike with fantastic gearing, complete with two computers on my handlebars that are connected to the world. Phileas Fogg, eat your heart out!

As the date of my ride loomed ever closer, I realised that all the thoughts I was having were not about other people, simply a reflection of me and my own perceived lack of action when I knew I could be doing so much more with my time on earth. When people tell me this ride is impressive, I really don't believe it is that special. I'm just privileged enough to be in a position to be able to do it. As I get older and less mobile, I will rue the opportunities I missed with no chance to go back and make amends. You will never be as young again as you are today, Craig. Make the most of it.

People wanted to chit-chat more about the ride with me as April the 19th started approaching. I was bored of talking about it; it had been in my life for many years and had consumed the past few months; I just wanted to get on with it. And I was still getting lots of advice.

'Oh, is that what I should do, is it? I'll scrap the months of research and planning I've put in based on a quick thought you've had. Yes, I'll be sure to mention you in my thank you speech about how I couldn't have done it without your input. Have you ever even ridden a bike before?'.

These encounters encouraged me to squeeze the word 'solo' into conversations whenever I was asked about the ride. They also reminded me why the 'solo' bit had been a driving force for my recent and future career in cycling adventures. It was great that people were interested, but I was getting frustrated and just wanted to get going.

The week leading up to the final departure ended up being a wee bit stressful. Work was fine, I was on top of things, and my clients were excellent with me disappearing for three weeks. But, the furore around the first day was getting to me.

Firstly, despite organising things months in advance, my send-off from the charity headquarters got cancelled because of timing. I was somewhat disappointed, considering the effort I'd put in, and the fact that I had invited lots of people I then had to let down, but these things happen. I also got wind of a few people wanting to cycle with me from Basingstoke to Portsmouth. It was pressure I didn't need.

I didn't want to fret about anyone but myself on the first day. Worrying about people getting punctures or being left behind was something I could well do without. I just wanted to cycle, and to get to Portsmouth with enough time to catch my ferry.

In the end, I did what I tend to do in these circumstances and threw my toys out of the pram. I would just leave my house, on my own, and on my own terms. No fanfare, no waves goodbye; see you in three weeks!

The pressure lifted very quickly, and I was ready.

Day 1 - Basingstoke to Portsmouth

'This is a sixty-mile-an-hour road. You shouldn't be on it on a pushbike!'

That was the logic of the Jaguar driver, stopped, sitting in the middle of a country lane in his idling car as I nestled against the hedgerow, trying to stay on my bike. For once, I was restrained. It was almost too ludicrous to argue against. Every time I retorted, it was with a laugh. But it was only 10 miles more until I took a ferry ride to the continent, where I would find more pleasant drivers who didn't hate cyclists, I thought. Play it cool, Craig, play it cool.

It had been a good day, starting with a lovely casual morning and the feeling of having plenty of time on my hands, only for it to slide away quicker than Arsenal's European ambitions earlier in the same week. I'd made some last-minute changes to my bike setup, including two brand-new pannier bags, which had only arrived at 9am on the morning of my departure.

I didn't have a packing routine as of yet, so my loading regime was a bit haphazard and consisted of me repeating, out loud, the phrase, 'Have I packed that yet?' approximately 5,000 times.

I finally left home at 11am. This would leave me an hour to get to my partner Lorraine's house, around

10 miles away, for a quick stop. It wasn't a dramatic affair. No fanfare, no waves goodbye. I could have well been cycling to work apart from the 40kg of extra weight I had loaded.

As I wobbled out of the village, getting used to the balance of the bike, I couldn't quite come to terms with the fact that I would now be cycling all the way to Spain. I had to keep saying it out loud - 'You're cycling to Spain, Craig!'

'Spain!'

'Spain!'

It didn't help that the first few miles of cycling were, as usual, a bit stiff. Doubt is not the perfect thought to have mulling around your head less than 15 minutes into a 22-day ride with your legs feeling like lead.

I was leaving my hometown of Basingstoke, an old market town that had expanded faster than my waistline did in my forties since being designated as an overspill town in the 1960s. My parents, who had spilled out from London together in the late sixties, bought a house on a new estate close to Kings Furlong, on the site of an old Orchard. So, I've lived in the town my entire life and have become one of those old farts who say things like, 'I remember when Hatch Warren was all fields, and we used to go up there strawberry picking'.

Despite the local shopping centre, Festival Place, being flat and smooth - the ideal place to wear out your mobility scooter tyres - most journeys out of the town involve going up a hill. I had two steep ones to contend with in the first 10 miles that would test me riding with all the gear on board as I headed towards the village of Cliddesden.

My first destination was Ellisfield, a 'lumpy' route about 17km away. Lorraine was waiting for me at her house and would be cycling with me on the first day. We'd planned for me to escape Basingstoke and get to hers for a baguette (my food of choice on the whole trip) before heading down to Portsmouth together.

I managed to get over and down the first two hills better than expected and found myself at Lorraine's house within an hour, scoffing my lunch and making more adjustments to the bike, having just had my first real ride fully loaded. My newly fitted pannier bags were much roomier than the ones I had replaced, so I decided that I could remove the rear rack bag, which had my tent bag balancing on top tied down with bungees. By ditching it, the tent bag sat more securely on the frame, and Terence now had more balance than a yogi. Good lad.

According to the weather report, the wind would be behind us on the ride down to Portsmouth, with the promise of a cloudy and sunny afternoon. Wind very rarely seems to be behind you on a bike, though. When it is, you don't tend to notice it, putting any extra speed gain down to your own stamina, right to the point when you have to turn into the wind and suddenly realise how much gain you were actually getting. As for the promised sunny afternoon, the gentle spitting soon turned into a downpour, and we found ourselves, quite literally, cycling upstream on a hill south of Alton. It was a sign of things to come.

The rolling Hampshire hills west of Petersfield rolled mainly upwards, and we were challenged with a 9% climb just west of Queen Elizabeth Park, as Lorraine took full advantage of a bike with one half-filled bag loaded on its pannier frame. I found it a little more challenging. Then, it was a case of rolling down the other side, past my lovely, new friend in his Jag, and onto the busy roads of Cosham before hitting Portsmouth.

I've cycled into Portsmouth before and recognised the busy route as we crossed over the junction with the M27, weaving through the traffic as cars darted on and off the roundabout as quickly as they could with the Friday rush hour looming. I just hoped there wasn't an angry Jaguar driver nearby; he'd probably make a beeline straight for me.

Holding onto the handlebars tightly and holding my nerve even tighter, I made it across unscathed, joining the final stretch of the A3 into the city. As luck would have it, Strava quickly guided us off the busy city road and onto the Hilsea Shore Path to join the dog walkers and the joggers enjoying the sun, which had finally decided to make an appearance with us nearly at our destination.

We had time on our side and stopped for a breather next to the South Coast Wakepark to watch wetsuited thrillseekers flying into the air on their wakeboards, holding on for dear life as the pulley system pulled them towards large ramps before they unceremoniously slapped back down onto the water struggling, and often failing, to remain on their feet.

The path led us down into the city and back out further on the A3, which had now become a much smaller and quieter road as it neared its final destination from London. The road flowed into a one-way system, with large cyclist signs painted on the tarmac to warn drivers they had to share the road. Luckily, they did, and we rode the last couple of kilometres to our destination for the day. Although we nearly missed it. It turns out that there are two pubs called The Ship & Castle in Portsmouth. Luckily, by just so happening to stop for a quick chat on the bikes, we realised we were heading for the wrong one just before I continued cycling an extra 2.5km past the correct one, which sat right next to the port.

We'd made it. The first day was done, and we rolled into a friendly little 'workers' pub right by the docks, made all the more working class with crates of racing pigeons being stacked out the front, readied for transport 'up north', just so that they could fly back down again tomorrow. We do have some strange pastimes in this country.

My friends, Rob and Jane, had driven down to wave me off and take Lorraine back home in the car, and we sat chatting in the pub, discussing our individual love and hate for salad cream. Rob and Jane talked about Bordeaux, having just taken a trip there. The city would be my first day off stop six days later.

I munched on a pie and chips, sipped my pint (of Coke), and let everyone else do the talking. My mind was elsewhere, mulling over the uncertainty of the next few weeks. I also felt confident I'd made a strong case for why Salad Cream is and always will be the best sauce in the condiments cupboard.

Then, it was time for goodbyes. Both Lorraine and me were trying to stay strong for each other, knowing that this was it. She is my rock and has seen me go through all the ups and downs of organising this ride, so she shared my anguish. If there was anyone who I would listen to and ask, it was her. I'd miss her a lot. There were a couple of trembling words in there as we bid our farewells, holding back any tears. Well, I know there were from me. We had a final hug, and then I cycled off into the evening, preparing myself for the unknown.

Lorraine had told me that she'd picked this pub as it was close to the ferry terminal. She wasn't wrong, and one hundred metres later, I was staring at large overhead signs to see what lane I should be in as I entered the terminal.

I've been on ferries before, even on a bike, but not on a bike on my own. A steward motioned for me to queue up with the cars at the check-in. Of course, I got in line behind the one car that got held up. Being on a push bike, though, if you're stuck behind the person who probably forgot their passport, you simply cycle across to an empty lane. I felt like a winner on two wheels as I picked up my ticket and cycled away while the car in the next lane was still stranded. Then, I was shepherded into another queue for bikes to wait in line with everyone else, eroding that winning feeling quite quickly.

It was so much easier than I had expected (that ended up being a running theme of my trip, by the way). All the uncertainties of the ferry procedure faded. I'd obviously overlooked the fact that these people deal with cyclists every single day.

I got chatting with four guys on bikes who had joined me in the two-wheel queue. Two of them got bored straight away, then another, and I was left speaking to one. He was French. They were heading out for a three-day cycle around Brittany and Normandy, and a couple of them looked a lot less prepared than their counterparts, wearing jeans and jumpers. But it's not a bad way to spend a long weekend, is it? And it was good to know I wasn't the only idiot on a bike in mid-April.

Then we were told to board the ferry, so we all pottered off following the flowing hand gestures of steward after steward across the concourse until arriving at the clattering ramp and the gaping steel entrance.

I love the car area on a ferry. It may be noisy and smell of exhaust fumes, but it just adds to the vibrant sight and sounds and sends me off on a nostalgic trip into my childhood and our family camping trips abroad, with me sitting in the middle of the back seat of the car between two elder brothers, both elbowing me to get more room.

I'd be full of excitement, stretching my neck out the front to take it all in as Dad was guided into a lane to park really, really close to the car in front by a person speaking in a strange language.

My mum would be busy asking, 'Could you three just bloody behave in the back?'. It was more of a demand.

We always took the midnight crossing from Dover to Calais as we headed off on our summer holidays, and it marked the beginning of some amazing camping trips across various places in Europe. It also meant I was allowed to run around a ship for ninety minutes in the middle of the night. Life doesn't get any better when you're nine.

As we were ushered to a side room at the front of the boat with our bikes, I knew that I still needed to sort out my pannier bag routine, especially with the brand-new additions. I tried very hard to look like I knew what I was doing in front of the other cyclists as I awkwardly removed the rear bags from Terence before leaving him with his two-wheeled comrades for the overnight journey.

Finding my cabin was fun. There I was, a big, sweaty oaf wearing cycling gear, helmet still on, lugging heavy pannier bags up steep stairs, trying to dodge people standing still and debating which way to go. 'It's the next level, Maureen, that's the bloody engine room. Just keep going up! Maureen… Maureen… I'm telling you, it's the next level!'.

As I finally emerged onto the cabin deck, I was feeling a little smug. I had paid extra and booked a cabin with a window view, and I was excited to see what wonders lay ahead. A large, luxury cabin like the one in the movie Titanic, perhaps? Maybe a tiny balcony to wave goodbye to Blighty? I carried on down corridor after corridor, edging towards the front of the boat and mingling with other people looking as equally confused as me, trying to locate their rooms. The numbering system was complicated, to say the least. I'm sure it made sense to someone when they designed it, but, in the cold light of day, it would have left a travelling Rachel Riley scratching her head.

I finally found my room, strangely not down one side of the boat, but in the middle facing forwards. I put down my heavy bags and opened the door to my luxury cabin.

It was tiny. There were two stick-thin single beds, and I dropped my bags onto the flimsy sheets of one, eager to see my window view. I shuffled sideways through the small gap down the middle of the room between the beds, straight to the window and did the classic double-handed, synchronised reveal, pulling back the curtains.

There was a big block of steel about one metre from the window and no sea to be seen unless I stretched my neck like an excited nine-year-old on the back seat of a family car entering the car deck down below.

It didn't take long to overcome the disappointment. I had a warm shower, which was very welcome after the day of wet and windy cycling. Then, it was time to wander towards the bar as the ship left the dock, drifting gently through the channel and out to open sea. The Spinnaker tower passed us gently by, as did the historic HMS Victory and HMS Warrior. I was on my way to France, and a pint of beer beckoned.

As I entered the bar, I immediately felt like I'd already made it to Benidorm. Exuberant groups of lads and couples sat around small tables full of booze, with empty glasses already stacking up. They were certainly taking full advantage of the drinking time between England and France as they settled down for a night of entertainment.

An overly enthusiastic compere was trying to get revellers at each table to join an upcoming quiz. Watching him work, I can only assume he must question his career choices every single night, especially halfway through round four - the food round - when people are already bored and ignoring him asking a question about cheese.

I sat nursing a pint, people-watching, wondering if anyone ever drove off the boat in the morning and straight into the sea.

'It's okay, officer. I've had a couple of hours kip and haven't had a drink since last night, monsieur. Not sure what went wrong there.'

I messaged Lorraine to tell her I had made it the extra few metres since I last saw her and was safe and sound, then it was back to my room and my new stretching regime - which was fun in the confines of a tiny ferry cabin (window or no window).

Stretching complete and my diary entry written, I settled down on the slither of a bed, ready for a good night's sleep. But, despite a strenuous day, sleep just didn't come. I tossed and turned all night - as best I could with the room I had available, which wasn't much. It was like wearing a straight jacket. My slumber wasn't helped by my phone announcing the arrival of a text message around 1am wishing me luck on my travels.

I'd only travelled 50 miles, some of which was by boat, but at least people back home were thinking of me. My adventure had truly begun.

67.1km down.

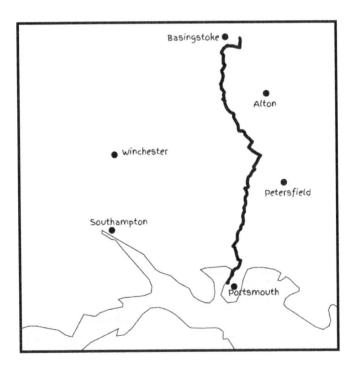

Day 2 - Saint-Malo To Rennes

'Cycle on the right, cycle on the right!'

I hadn't slept at all well with the constant hum of the engine and a million and one irrational thoughts rushing through my head all night long.

After a few hours of squirming, I checked my phone to see the time, but I couldn't get a signal. It was the only reference I had to the time of day (and night), and being cut off, I couldn't pinpoint whether the clock had changed the one hour forward as we neared the continent. Was it 5:30am, or was it 4:30am? Needless to say, this was just another thing to add to the merry-go-round in my brain, so I finally got up for a wander, not really knowing what the time was.

I've become a very early riser in recent years, something I thought only old people did. Maybe I am ahead of my time? Or, perhaps I am just already old and don't want to admit it out loud.

As I walked around a ghostly quiet boat, it turned out the clock had changed. People who hadn't chosen a cabin for the overnight journey slept across floors and between seats, including, it turns out, my cycling buddies from the terminal. I was at least grateful to have had the chance to shower after a wet and sweaty day rather than having to sleep in my clothes.

I found a coffee machine, so life was okay as I sat staring out at the ocean. I felt exhausted, but at the same time, I was feeling energised by the anticipation of the next part of my journey.

When the breakfast area finally opened, with the boat starting to show signs of life, I got myself a pain au chocolat. And, of course, I had more coffee. It made me proud to be British, standing behind a fellow countrywoman in the queue, listening as she loudly and clearly asked for her breakfast in English with no recognition whatsoever that the menu was in French and that the staff were French.

Before long, it was time to disembark. I just hoped I could remember my way back down to the car deck from my room as I trundled back through the myriad of corridors with my heavy bags, wearing my helmet like a badge of honour - 'Yes, I am cycling, thank you, please step aside.'

I jumped the gun as the speaker announced who could and couldn't return to the car deck, dodging past people blocking the stairwells, including Maureen still arguing with her husband about which level they were on, with me trying not to bash into excited young children running around with no parental control on display.

Despite ignoring the call to wait my turn, when I arrived at the bike room, I was one of the last cyclists to return to prepare my bike. Terence had been moved by another eager rider, and I bumbled my new bags back onto the frame, still with no clear routine, skill, or aptitude for knowing what I was doing, as people came and went with their own bikes.

Eventually, all ready and set to go, the cyclists were waved off through the giant mouth of the ferry before all the frustrated (and possibly still drunk) drivers looked on bleary-eyed from their cars. I was in France.

Unsure of what to do, I just followed the other cyclists across the large concourses, unenthusiastically directed by the French stewards in the fresh morning weather. After some slow cycling across the docks, we arrived at the empty customs queue, cars still well behind us, and I passed through quickly, my new blue passport gaining yet another stamp. Having a record of my trip was nice, but I'd still much prefer a red one.

I said 'Au Revoir' to my French ami and his English friends and cycled away, reminding myself to cycle on the right-hand side of the road - I'd like to make it further than the first roundabout on this journey. My computer told me to take the first right turn and head south.

But, in the distance, to my left, was the walled city of Saint-Malo. If I was going to make the most of this ride, I couldn't just ride away and ignore it. So, I decided to pay no attention to my computer and turned left - making sure I turned right to go anti-clockwise around the roundabout first.

Bonjour, I said to my four cycling friends who had taken the same route, heading towards the walled city, and as we approached the imposing structure, I started looking to find the best way to get to the other side, to penetrate the citadel. It would be a great chance to grab a coffee and take in the surroundings. Although I had 75km planned for the day, it was still early, so I had plenty of time to play with.

I took the first road through the ancient city brick defence and soon found myself wobbling vigorously over empty, cobbled streets. I'm cycling in a French city, I thought, and on cobbles. It was exciting.

I made my way through to busier-looking streets, and still, there was no open café to be found. Had it been worth the diversion, after all?

I stumbled out of yet another street junction, starting to feel dejected, and there it was, Place Chateaubriand and the imposing St. Vincent Gate. It was as French as French could be, with the added bonus of having not one, but five cafés to choose from. My dejection disappeared quicker than you could say, 'un café, s'il vous plait'.

I parked Terence at an outside table (no one was sitting outside at this time of day; it was still a cold 8:30am) and popped my head in through the door, asking for 'un café'. Then I went back to sit next to Terence to keep him company, and to make sure no one stole him. That being said, I'm not so sure anyone would have been able to run that fast across the cobbles with Terence and his load.

About three minutes later, a waiter finally came out of the empty café; I thought to bring my lovely warm coffee, but no, to ask me what I would like.

'Un café', I said again.

When it arrived a few minutes later, I asked for the bill straightaway so I could shoot off without waiting as soon as I was finished. It was also the moment when I realised that 'un café' is an espresso. I'd need to brush up on my coffee-asking French phrases if I wanted a longer black coffee.

Despite spending five years learning French at senior school, my knowledge is very sketchy, especially when you throw in the preceding 32 years. For instance, I could tell you in French that I am 11 years old and I live in Basingstoke. And, for some reason, I could also tell you that I got up this morning at 5:30am, but apart from that, I would be relying on Google translate quite a lot over the next ten days unless anyone just happened to want to know where Monsieur Lafayette was, in which case I could tell them that he is in the garden with the brown cat.

As I sat, pondering in the cold square with my warm shot of coffee, and with the smell of the sea never too far away, a large flock of seagulls floated around a very blue morning sky, making the loud noise that only seagulls can make. Signs of life were starting to appear, as tourists, possibly foot passengers from the same ferry I'd just arrived on, wandered confused, looking at their phones, I assumed, following directions to a hotel. It's quite amusing watching someone trying to push a suitcase with wheels one-handed across a cobbled street while trying to understand what a 'rue' is.

Despite the pull of an intriguing sign pointing me in the direction of the Saint-Malo Micro Zoo, I thought I'd better crack on and do some cycling. I still wonder to this day which animals could possibly be in a micro zoo and how small a micro zoo could actually be.

Terence bounced across the cobbles, and we exited through St. Vincent Gate and out onto boring, smooth, tarmac-covered roads as I tried to find my way south and out of the city. My computer told me to go back the way I'd come. It was quicker and easier, no doubt, but I never seem to want to retrace my route if I can help it, another running theme to my cycling adventure.

Being at sea level, I knew I'd be going up out of Saint-Malo to begin my morning, and my cold legs slowly started to warm up through the stiffness as I edged my way out onto country roads, still marvelling at the experience. Once again, I reminded myself I was actually on the trip I'd been planning for all these years.

Long, straight roads allowed me to get through some distance quite quickly, but it was starting to get boring. Terence was also making a worrying noise. I had recently had to replace the bottom bracket on the bike - the bit that goes through the frame by the peddles - and this sounded like the same issue re-occurring. Despite the bike being just over a year old, when Graham (my awesome local bike mechanic from Pukka Bikes) changed the original one out, which had developed a loud 'clacking' noise (technical term), he showed me the piece of metal, complete with plastic holders still on it, which made us discuss how Terence must have been a Friday afternoon bike. For the younger readers, this is the old idea that you've ended up with a machine that was put together on a Friday afternoon after the factory workers had been down the pub for a pint to two and just wanted the weekend to come, lackadaisically seeing out their afternoon tasks.

I panicked, messaged Graham, and hoped it wouldn't get worse. To his credit, he was straight on it, ordering a new one, just in case, which he sent out with Lorraine to Bordeaux a week later, complete with all the tools I'd need to change it. Top man.

As lunchtime approached, and the roads remained long and tedious, I stopped in the square at Tinténiac, a small town halfway along my route towards Rennes. Opting for the Tabac shop, rather than the much nicer looking boulangerie and bistro, I scoffed my first French Baguette, along with another 'un café' (on purpose this time) and a Coke, and looked at what lay ahead for the afternoon's riding. It was a cool day, but the rain had held off, and the sky was blue. So far, so good.

Rather than remove my bike computer - which was a full two metres away from where I was sitting - I consulted Google Maps on my phone to see how far I had left to ride for the day.

That can't be right! That's 15km longer than I was expecting!

Google had created a cycling route, but it wasn't the one I was on. This one was along the side of a nearby canal, less than 100 metres away from where I was sitting.

It looked flatter than the route I had left to do. Should I continue on the boring straight and 'lumpy' roads, or opt for the winding Canal d'Ille-et-Rance all the way to Rennes?

Ten minutes later, I hit the gravel path of the canal, congratulating myself for being spontaneous.

It's worth re-iterating that spontaneity is not one of my strong points, and one of the reasons for my trip was to challenge myself to go off-piste a little. In reality, I was in no great rush to get to my campsite, so why not switch it up and move off the boring roads?

It turned out to be a fantastic decision, and I rode beside the meandering waterway all the way to Betton, on the outskirts of Rennes, around 8km away from my stop for the night - the municipal campsite, nestled in the heart of the Parc des Gayeulles in the North-East of the city.

It made such a difference to my afternoon and was in complete contrast to my morning. I rode around pretty locks, smiling at the nonchalant barge drivers chugging along slowly. I practised my singing 'bonjours' at the passing cyclists and walkers out enjoying the sunny Saturday afternoon. I stopped by a lake to shoot some video on my drone to document my ride. It was such a contrast to my day in Hampshire, just the day before.

But as I got closer to the city, the happy 'bonjours' ceased, and I had to start navigating my way through city folk walking dogs or taking up the width of the path in large groups. They didn't seem quite as accommodating at having to share the trail with a cyclist as the people I'd come across earlier in my day.

Not that I am paranoid, but it probably didn't help that I looked English, something I never seemed able to escape, no matter how cool I'd like to look. I'd love to have the air of a suave European, but I don't. I could be wearing a linen shirt, slacks and some espadrilles with the arms of a sailing jumper over my shoulders, and I'd still look like I've just been shopping at M&S for new socks and pants.

I consoled myself with the beautiful route I had ridden all afternoon. Cycling routes in France are far superior to those in the UK and a dream to ride on. We're not just stuffed onto the edge of a busy road with glass, rubble and broken tarmac, trying to cycle around parked cars. There are paths designed explicitly around cyclists, and I rode through a few kilometres of a dedicated cycle route on the edge of Rennes, sponsored by the sports brand Decathlon, with not a car in sight. It was lovely.

My own private cycleway led me through to the edge of the Parc des Gayeulle, and I veered off to make my way through tight tracks around the back of the woodland walks and down towards the entrance to the campsite.

It was around 4:30pm. The sun was shining, there was a clear blue sky, and it was surprisingly warm. I was the first to arrive and check-in for the overnight camping and had the pick of the pitches, so I unpacked and started to set up my tent.

Half an hour or so later, a woman I had passed on the canal earlier in the day turned up on her bike. Perhaps slightly older than me, it was great to see another more mature rider. She parked up her electric bike, which was pulling a small bike trailer, and started to unpack her tent a couple of pitches down from where I'd set up.

Meanwhile, having set up my tent and sufficiently pottered, an essential part of the camping experience, I left my new neighbour laying out her tent and headed to the shower block to wash myself and my clothes.

When I returned 20 minutes later, she was struggling to put her tent up, with one hand on a pole and the other holding her phone on a video call to a man with a very deep voice. Chatting away in French, I think she and the person on the other end of the call were trying to work out why her poles would not fit the tent, a slight sense of concern etched on her face.

I watched from afar and thought this could be my chance to be helpful and friendly. But I was torn. Should I be chivalrous, or should I remember it's 2024, where it's often frowned upon, and women don't need men, thank you very much! I didn't want to be seen to be mansplaining (or should I say hommeexpliquant?) if it wasn't welcome.

In the end, I couldn't help myself and went across to help. I would have done it if it were a man, so what difference would it make that she was a woman? It turned out she was incredibly grateful, and she nodded vigorously as we communicated in a garbled conversation while I looked at the tent and the poles.

'Oui, chérie', I said in my best patronising man-voice, 'You are putting the poles into the tent the wrong way around'. It had taken ten seconds to figure out. (Rest assured, I didn't say that at all.)

I had a new friend as we continued to raise her shelter together. It turned out she had borrowed the tent from a friend. Half the pegs were missing, and let's just say it was a tent that had seen better days, many years ago. I knew how it felt.

'You should have done what I did, mon amie, and bought loads of brand new stuff online that you'll only ever use once, maybe twice, then spend the next five years tripping over it in the garage!'

As the sun slowly lowered towards the tree line, one more person cycled into the small camping area. He was on a mountain bike and was carrying very little luggage. Having leant his bike on a tree, he just sat in the middle of his camping pitch, looking at his phone. How cool is he, I thought. He's there, not a care in the world. The tent can wait. He's so laid-back.

It wasn't until later that I realised he just had a bivvy bag, which is just like a large thick sleeping bag. No need for a tent (and the extra microns of nylon it offers you for protection) for this chap.

With Terence locked up, my damp washing drying in the evening sun, which was also feeding my travel solar power unit, the evening felt young. It was only six o'clock, and I wanted some food.

Having enquired at the reception, I walked down through the campsite, out to the park and towards a restaurant by the lake. It was a sunny Saturday evening and it seemed that half of the city of Rennes had made the same choice. Most of them had also decided to congregate around the bar and restaurant area, with a DJ playing music that was really not conducive to a relaxing evening in a park.

I felt a little out of place and quite intimidated. That happens quite a lot to me, even at the age of 53. So I walked out towards the park's main entrance to see what was available in the surrounding streets. The quick answer, I discovered, was not a lot. I found a petrol garage, bought some crisps, biscuits and a couple of beers and headed back to the campsite.

My French neighbour had retreated to her tent, which was luckily still standing, in as much as the Leaning Tower Of Pisa is still standing. My hardened mountain biker friend was still sitting cross-legged, looking at his phone. I passed an empty pitch with a toothbrush just lying in the grass. Some people are so lackadaisical, I thought as I headed to my little patch of grass.

The sun had now fully crept behind the trees and taken its warmth well and truly with it, as well as its solar energy to recharge my panels. It was getting very cold very quickly. So I packed away my kit, took down my washing and retreated to my tent with my make-shift dinner. To say it was cosy would be like saying a wetsuit has a little bit of give. I soon realised that my movement would be very limited in the tent, similar to a bed in a ferry cabin but complete with a nylon cage surrounding me.

I also realised that there would be no way for a man of my size and age to be able to get in and out of this tent with any grace or dignity, reminding me of the time I once had to borrow my girlfriend's little Mazda sports car to pop into town. When I tried to get out of it, I had to roll out sideways onto the floor. This wouldn't have been so bad if I hadn't been in a busy car park with coins noisily escaping from my pocket, rolling under the car next to me, as passers-by watched on in amusement.

I managed to get some football commentary on my phone and climbed into my sleeping bag. It felt so warm and cosy that I dozed through half the match. I was understandably tired and couldn't wait to close my eyes and recharge my body.

My problem was that it didn't quite happen like that. I could not get comfortable. My travel air bed was wafer thin. I also didn't have two pillows like I do at home, so my arms had nowhere to go. I am not entirely sure what I do with my arms at home in bed, but it works and I sleep well. In the tent, I kept getting pins and needles. If, for any reason, in the middle of the night, I had to make an emergency exit, I'd be buggered, rolling around the floor like a worm, not being able to sit, stand or exit with style, with my arms dangling down like half-filled balloons in the wind. I guess I'd just have to roly-poly myself to safety, trying not to knock down my neighbour's fragile home on the way.

As the night wore on, it was also getting colder and colder. I put my trousers on. Then I put my fleece on. Then I put two extra pairs of socks over the two pairs I was already wearing. Then I just waited for the night to be over, wiggling my fingers in the air, trying to bring my arms back to life.

It wasn't the best start to my camping adventure.

91.3km for the day - 158.4km travelled.

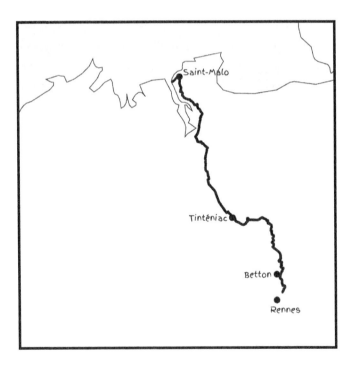

Day 3 - Rennes to Ancenis

A coffee, a coffee, my kingdom for a coffee...
And a Burger.

Have you ever had one of those nights where you lie, tossing and turning, your mind running away with itself, just willing morning to arrive? How about two nights on the trot? Despite being exhausted from a lack of sleep on the ferry the night before, followed by a complete day of cycling, once again, it just didn't happen.

My broken sleep snapped like a dry twig very early in the morning when I realised the tent was damp. It hadn't rained, so I could only guess that the heat from my body had been drawn out, like a soul being sucked out by a Dementor, only to find the thin nylon sheet so impenetrable that it decided to set up shop there and form small droplets of condensation.

When the darkness finally started to lift, so did my sense of relief that the night was over. It still felt far too early to rise, and I was too cold to even think about roly-polying out of the tent, so I decided to just lay there with my sleeping bag tucked tightly over my chins for a short while. The Sun had still not broken the treeline and I was still freezing, but eventually, I summoned the courage to remove my arms from the warm cocoon and tease down the zip of the inner tent lining, placing my hand on the outer skin of my overnight accommodation. It was soaking wet. It also felt crispy, of all things, so I undid the second zip. The grass was covered with a gentle layer of frost, like someone had carefully spray-painted the tips of each blade white. I poked out my arm and reached around to discover a huge clue as to why I was so bloody cold. The tent was covered in small patches of ice.

As I lay there, tired, cold and miserable, I decided to break with my plan of camping again that night, using my phone to book a hotel for the next destination. I really needed some comfort and a good night's sleep and I soon found a room 108km away in Ancenis-Saint-Géréon.

It was 7:30am as I finally poked my head out of the tent like a tortoise, looking for signs of life while clinging to my sleeping bag for dear life, shuffling sidewards toward the damp opening. First, across to my French lady neighbour whose tent had managed to stay up through the night despite a severe lack of pegs. Then, over to the young cyclist opposite me, lying dead still in his bag, which resembled a small coffin on the large campsite pitch. He wasn't moving a muscle. I kept staring. I couldn't see any rise and fall. Despite the sub-artic temperatures, I also couldn't see any steamy breath floating above the top of the bag. I started to wonder if he'd frozen solid in the middle of the night.

The thought of the long day ahead and the desperate need for a steaming cup of hot coffee shook me into action, and I gingerly slid out of my sleeping bag, still fully clothed. Then I pondered how on earth I was going to get out of the tent, keeping my feet dry. Stiff as a board all over, legs like lead, it felt like the challenge of my life, and I spent far too much time thinking about it. Eventually, I just hopped out of the tent, trying to put on my shoes, hopping around with the grace of an old Russian drunkard.

First things first, I unpacked my small gas cooker, folding out the heating element from its pouch and screwing it onto the gas bottle. A little bit of wiggling to get some balance and a pot of cold water went onto the hot stand as I placed my hands around the welcome burst of heat.

It was at that very moment, like a bolt from the blue, that the caffeine rug was well and truly pulled from under my frozen feet with the realisation that I had forgotten my coffee dripper! An inverted cone-shaped plastic device that sits on the cup with a paper filter to fill with ground coffee, it was essential to transform plain old water into wake-up juice, and I was buggered without it.

I knew I'd forget something on this trip, and this was it. Despite repeating my 'Have I packed that yet?' mantra several times when I was getting ready, I could suddenly picture it clearly, standing proud on my kitchen side at home. Let's face it, forgetting a dripper is better than forgetting a passport or a wallet, but this one tiny oversight meant I ended up having a tepid cup of water and some leftover biscuits for breakfast.

'Let it go, Craig, and crack on.' My new mantra kicked in, and with a full day of cycling ahead of me, I grabbed my wash bag and headed for the toilet block to get a quick wash and brush my teeth. After the damp walk across the grass, I opened my washbag in front of the metal sink unit. Bugger, I'd only gone and lost my toothbrush as well. Not the best start to the day!

Hang on a minute, that toothbrush I saw on the grass last night, the one left by a complete idiot. It didn't half look like mine!

Now, I'm not sure if the ten-second rule only applies to food, or if it can be extended to toothbrushes, or, if the ten seconds can be extended to ten hours. Whatever the answers to these age-old conundrums, five minutes later, I was busy brushing my teeth with a very cold toothbrush, picking bits of grass out of my mouth.

It took me a lot longer than I expected to pack up and leave, trying to understand what thing went in what bag and wondering how dry I could get my tent without getting anything else too wet. It turns out that the answers to the two puzzles were not much and no chance.

I finally rolled out of the campsite at 9:30am, dying for a coffee and hoping the breakfast of water and biscuits would suffice until I found somewhere to get a hot drink and something more substantial to give me the energy I'd need for the day.

I was certainly not in the mood for sightseeing, which was just as well, as skirting around Rennes city centre didn't lend itself to wonderful vistas and squares with bistros enticing me in. I'm probably being unfair, but as if to prove a point - after dodging some very heavy and aggressive traffic with drivers who obviously didn't get Lionel Richie's memo that Sundays should be easy - I found myself in an industrial estate as I left the city heading south.

My legs were stiff, and my kneecaps had started to ache. This was a brand new pain after two solid days of cycling and not a welcome one. The first thought that came to mind was something my sports massage therapist had said a few weeks earlier when she asked me outright if I had any pains in my kneecaps, as if this was something terrible, indicating that my legs might fall off very soon. I'd just have to grin and bear it and expect at least some pain in my knees from the constant cycling during the day, and balancing on very thin beds at night.

Through a large sports complex on a lovely little cycle path, I was soon crossing a long, arched bridge over the N136, part of the motorway network which circles the city, before joining a series of lanes and paths alongside the D173, a busy dual carriageway.

It wasn't the most fun way of making distance, but at least I could see the kilometres ahead falling away. And, despite being hungry, at least I'd warmed up a bit.

I could see a town not far away on the map, perfect. Somewhere to stop and eat. But, when I arrived, now 16km into my day, Vern-sur-Seiche had nothing to offer, so I had to carry on.

Corps-Nud offered the same eight kilometres later, leaving me beginning to worry about sustenance for the rest of the day. The next big town was 38km away, so I carried on. I didn't really have a choice. Surely, I could carry on for another three hours on my breakfast biscuit ration, combined with my current store of fat deposits.

Eventually, the town of Châteaubriant was within touching distance. Despite the difference in spelling and bearing no relevance whatsoever, the thought of a beautiful, moist steak filled my mind, sending me off remembering a Chateaubriand I had eaten back in the late noughties at a local posh hotel. It's amazing where your mind goes on a bike, and I never really understand why people choose to block the inane chattering and meandering river of thoughts that come with cycling, or indeed walking or running, by stuffing in some earbuds.

In a world where the phrase' mental health' gets bandied around like a badge of honour, I always find that a good walk or an hour on the bike lets me clear my mind and improve my mental resilience.

Mental resilience is a much better phrase to be using, in my opinion, because it's about control. Mental health suggests outsourcing blame and looking for drugs; resilience is something you can build upon in your own way if you switch off and allow your mind to process the shit you generate upstairs in your head.

That said, I was still only on day three, so I'd yet to tackle any big, thoughtful subjects and was happy to just keep thinking about food as I pictured a big plate of fries, followed by a nice pastry and a coffee.

As I entered the town, starting to flag and desperate for carbs, I aimed for the 'centre-ville'. There must be something here! As I rolled into a square in the town, four hours and 60km of cycling under my belt already for the day, a sense of tired relief overcame me as I saw a brasserie with someone sitting outside nursing un café. Bingo.

I parked Terence up, packed away my English shyness, and walked through the door.

Now, you know when you see a building that looks lovely from the outside, but, when you open the door, it doesn't quite have the same vibe and every head turns your way? Well, Bonjour to that! If someone had been playing a piano in the corner of the bar, they would've stopped dead to add extra tension.

As quickly as everyone started staring at me, they stopped, heading back to their busy conversations or the football match on the small TV above the bar, and I was left there dazed as to what had just happened.

In my broken French, I asked the barman if he had any 'mangé'. He caught my drift by thinking for approximately a 10th of a second before nonchalantly replying, 'Non!' like only a Frenchman can. Great! Four hours of cycling and still no food.

'Is there anywhere near to eat? Get food?' I asked, pushing my hand towards my mouth as if I was stuffing rice into my face. He understood and started thinking.

This time, he stretched to a full second. 'Non!'

I still had 48km to ride and felt as flat as a pancake. Day three was proving to be my nemesis.

I ordered 'un café' so that I could sit and ruminate.

Sunday in France is like an old-fashioned Sunday as a kid in Basingstoke. Things actually shut, and the world feels like it is on pause. Back on those long, long Sundays, all there was to do was watch re-runs of Little House On The Prairie in the morning and hope that at least one of my friends was allowed out to play in the afternoon. Of course, that would involve having to go and knock for them all one by one to find out, which also managed to waste some of the day, even if they weren't coming out.

That nostalgia didn't help me now, though. I could, I supposed, cycle around the town a bit, hoping that something else was open. But, like a quintessentially gullible Englishman, I took the barman for his word.

I didn't stay in the bistro for long. I would just have to crack on and get where I was going. The sooner I got to the hotel, the sooner this day would be over.

Back with my old pal Terence, I pilfered my bags and found a Tracker Bar I had brought with me from home. What seemed like an unnecessary 30 grammes at the time was suddenly coming to my rescue. Then, feeling despondent, we rolled out of the square.

My energy was low, and I was not looking forward to the rest of the day. I would just have to refer to Cycling Rule Number Five (look it up if you don't know).

Two minutes later, my head still firmly down, I joined the main road heading out of the town south. That's when I saw it - a gigantic billboard for Burger King. The enormous red arrow pointing up to the sky told me it was just two minutes away in a car on this very road and that it was open seven days a week.

When I got there, thanking every Lord available, there was a huge McDonald's right next door. It may not be French Cuisine, but it was food. I had half a mind to roll back into Dodge City, shoot the imaginary piano player in the corner of the bar, grab the barman by the scruff of the neck, pause for a full second and, through gritted teeth, push out the word, 'Oui!'

Instead, despite the self-service kiosk explaining the bright pictures of food on offer in French, I managed to order some sort of burger, fries, and a big fat Coke. Did I want to go large? You bet I did.

I love self-serve machines in shops and fast-food restaurants; it means one less idiot to talk to during my day. That said, I don't do fast-food chains very often, and the menus seem to have become infinitely more complex than when I was young. Perhaps the same person who designs fast food menus also designs room numbering systems on ferries? There were all sorts of combinations available, along with wraps, salads and other non-burger based meals. I'm sure we only had about five burger choices in my day, and two of those didn't really count being chicken and fish.

I scoffed my meal, the only diner sitting outside in the miserable afternoon. A fast-food burger never tasted so good, this one bowing down to nationalism with French goat's cheese to give it some tang. My mood lightened instantly, and the afternoon 48km I had left suddenly didn't seem so daunting.

Although a little up and down, the distance disappeared quickly, with me, newly powered by burger, moving swiftly, skirting through the towns of Moisdon-la-Rivière, Riaillé and Teillé on the D14. I didn't see any more bars, bistros or shops - open or closed - until I hit Ancenis-Saint-Géréon, my destination for the night.

As the main road entered the edge of town, I stopped to put the hotel address into Google Maps on my phone. With it connected firmly to my handlebars, I would use this route to guide me directly to my home for the night.

The next few kilometres turned out to be my first experience of how bad Google is at offering cycle routes on the fly. Rather than cycling in on the same road I was on, I was guided into a housing estate and up small paths between back gardens before being popped out on the very same road I had been on a little way further up. I'd like to say I would learn from this experience, but I didn't.

The IBIS Styles hotel I had chosen was ideal. The man in reception was friendly and helpful, and there was a shed for Terence to rest in for the night. After two nights, one in a cabin and one in a tent, it felt good to have my own bathroom and a bed wider than my body. I also had heat, electricity and Wi-Fi.

Washed and changed, I headed out to get some food. Any restaurant would do, even another Burger King. I was that desperate. The man at the hotel reception suggested the centre of town for somewhere to eat, so I took a 20-minute stroll through some busy, ugly roads, including a tight path under a road tunnel, into the older part of the town centre where I could see shops and restaurants up ahead. They were all shut.

I carried on through and out of the centre of town, down towards the castle and the bridge over the expansive Loire River. My mind was distracted from my hunger as I stopped to take in the fact that I had cycled to the Loire Valley… On a bike… Just me. At moments like this - and they continued throughout my trip - I felt an enormous sense of achievement. As much as it would have been great to share it with someone, it was also nice to enjoy the solitary moment and appreciate the months of planning and training I'd put in to make it happen. Yes, I made it all about me.

I noticed an open bar on the other side of the road, running parallel to the river, so I walked back over to check it out. A beer may have to suffice for my calorie intake this evening. I could see people sitting outside under cover, but I wasn't sure if I was meant to sit down and wait for a waiter to arrive or not.

Gingerly, I walked towards the bar entrance, which was buzzing with people inside enjoying food and drink and each other's company.

I wasn't sure about protocol, and someone was getting turned away at the door. Should I just sit at a table outside and wait? The way bars work on the continent seems to have changed over the years with the advent of mobile card payment machines. Gone are the days when you just sat down and, within seconds, a waiter appeared like the shopkeeper in Mr Benn.

In the past, I lacked confidence in social situations like this and would often feel out of my depth and just walk away. It's a self-conscious flaw I've worked hard to overcome over the years, and one of the reasons for me making this trip was to keep wedging me out of my comfort zone. In years gone by, I may well have walked away, but when the waiter came out, I simply caught his attention and asked if I could sit outside. It sounds so simple on paper, but we all know those emotions of uncertainty can be crippling, especially when language is a barrier.

Thankfully, unlike his compatriot I met earlier in the day, this particular Frenchman replied, 'Oui'. He also spoke some English, so I managed to order not just a beer, but having overheard the word saucisson, I reciprocated with my own 'oui', followed by a 's'il vous plait'.

Ten minutes later, I was sitting back relaxing, feeling somewhat smug with my coat done up all the way to the chin in the evening cold, sipping beer and popping fresh slices of spicy meat into my mouth with a knife like a Viking. It wasn't the largest plate of food, or the most balanced meal, but it did the job, and I slowly sauntered back to my hotel half and hour later with the meat sweats.

Of course, as I arrived back at my hotel, I noticed something I had missed entirely on the way out. Directly opposite, in a parade of shops, was an open bar serving food.

By then, I was so tired all I could offer was a small, meaty chuckle.

108km for the day - 266km travelled.

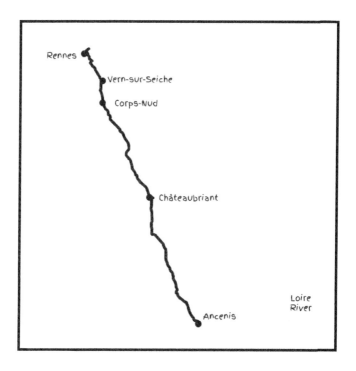

Day 4 - Ancenis to La Roche Sur Yon

'Enjoy your day and stay safe. When it feels tough, just remember I am in Milton Keynes working, and you are having an adventure!'

Man, I slept well. A proper double bed, complete with proper pillows to allow my arms to do their thing, meant my star fishing career could continue. I woke up renewed.

My legs felt stiff after three solid days of cycling, and my left knee was playing up, but apart from that, I was as good as new. I got out of bed, located my little spiky ball, wooden 'Tiger's Tail' and thick elastic band, and got straight to my stretching exercises to iron out my concrete legs.

For some reason, I also decided to re-plan my day ahead. The route looked quite hilly, and my throbbing knee was not enjoying the thought of pushing the weight of a loaded bike up a hill or ten. Sitting on my bed looking at maps on my computer while actually being on the ride, experiencing the terrain, and not just viewing it on my huge computer screen at home, made a big difference. I saw that I could change my destination by cycling southwest down the Loire Valley towards Nantes, then southwards to a town called La Roche Sur Yon. This would leave a much shorter day tomorrow and knock off a few hundred metres of climbing today. Running alongside a river would inevitably mean a morning of flat riding.

Feeling a sense of renewed optimism, I hit the buffet breakfast bar in the hotel restaurant. The food wasn't great, but there was plenty of it, plus warm coffee. After yesterday's debacle, it felt like an absolute feast. I wore my coat to the dining room so that I could make and take some extra breakfast rolls and pastries for the journey. After all, why keep paying for lunch when I can steal it for free? I know it's debatable etiquette, but I felt that, on balance, my charitable adventure supported the theft.

I liked being in a hotel - the bed, the lack of ice when you wake up, the breakfast laid out for you. So, I committed to doing it again that night, especially as the weather didn't look much warmer for later that evening. I'd leave it until lunchtime to see how I was getting on and then look for a hotel online.

Look at me! Mr. Spontaneity. I never thought I'd be that sort of person, but with the advent of booking.com, it all seemed quite easy, removing a lot of jeopardy.

I packed up Terence, improvising to make sure the bike was balanced. Then, I sent my newly planned (and much flatter) route for the day from my phone to my bike computer.

'Recalculating Elevation!' said the message on the screen. It flashed for a few seconds before explaining my day ahead in numbers, which now included an extra 1,000 metres of climbing compared to when I had planned it earlier this very morning on the computer. That can't be right, surely? I just hoped (prayed) that Strava on the computer was better than my Garmin bike computer at guessing ups and downs, because I wasn't sure my knees could take it today, of all days.

After the hardships of the day before, especially the lack of food, I just wanted today to go without incident. As if the cycling Gods were directly tuned in to 'Craig's Whinging FM', I was rewarded with the most glorious morning of cycling.

It never ceases to amaze me how you can use software on a computer (in this case, Strava), click on a destination 100km away, tell it you are on a bike, and off it goes, creating a route based on lots of other riders' past journeys, all in a matter of seconds. And to do it so much better than Google - the mother of all data scrapers - is the cherry on the cake.

As I left the hotel, I was guided this way and that, accidentally riding through a small car park before heading southwest out of the town onto some green country lanes that reminded me a lot of my local rides in leafy Hampshire.

On my computer screen, I could see water coming into view on the left-hand side of the display and the route in front of me edging closer towards it. And then, there it was, The Loire River, mercilessly drifting towards the Atlantic as it had for thousands of years, the morning sun shimmering over its wide, flowing expanse of clear blue.

I only realised once I returned home just how long the Loire River is. At a length of 1,006 kilometres, it starts its journey in the Massif Central and is the longest river in France, meandering through the middle of the country before entering the Atlantic around 85km west of where we'd met that morning.

The sun had made a welcome appearance, and the route was flat. I was enjoying flowing alongside the river, and so was my knee. The cycling itself was effortless, and I had the empty bike path on the river's north bank all to myself, sandwiched between the water on my left and a railway track to my right. The only inclines I encountered along the way were when the route dipped down to meet access tunnels under the tracks of the railway line. I would have enjoyed the rollercoaster-esque style of the path, except there were gates on either side of the dip, causing me to stop each time.

Every so often, I'd hear the electrical buzz of the tracks announcing the imminent passing of a train. It reminded me of the movie Back To The Future. But a DeLorean travelling 88 miles per hour on the track never showed, just a series of trains packed with bored commuters heading to Nantes.

Ten kilometres into my day, and it was time to cross over to the south side of the river. We take bridges for granted, but the power of this waterway made me reassess human ingenuity and how I'd be royally screwed without a road crossing at this point. I joined the cars and camper vans going about their business and sat tightly on the edge of the single-lane road, with a queue forming patiently behind me; a chubby bloke heading south, wobbling on a stacked bike, trying to video the river on his phone. What a knob!

Safely across on the other side, I took a quick stop to reply to a message from my friend Rob, who had asked how I was getting on. I sent him the video of the river I'd just taken. Luckily, he didn't just tell me to piss off. Instead, he graciously wished me well, mentioning that he was in Milton Keynes, working, and telling me to stay safe and have a great day.

Heading west, the route moved into a wooded area, the river now to my right behind a curtain of trees. The effort of whoever designed and created these glorious paths was not lost on me as I embraced the next stage of my cycling adventure, passing the odd cyclist and exchanging 'Bonjours'. It was beautiful. Much better than Milton Keynes.

The path continued, winding through the trees, which became gradually more sparse before I joined a quiet lane back alongside the mighty river heading to Nantes.

The road was smooth and flat, and I was making good progress. As I entered the small town of La Pierre Percée around mid-morning, I saw a choice ahead of me. I could stay on the road, which was set back from the river and would be much faster, or I could cycle down to the adjacent walkway running alongside the river and enjoy my continuing journey down the winding Loire. As enticing as the road was, I chose the more picturesque route and enjoyed the pathway alongside the river for the next nine kilometres.

The day wasn't particularly hot, but the sun was out, and I even managed to take my jacket off and enjoy some nice weather for the first time on my trip.

It was a memorable morning, and I knew Nantes was coming, where I'd need to head south. It was time to say goodbye to the Loire. Cycling away from the water, crossing over a busy intersection, I joined a cycle path next to the busy dual carriageway of the N844 heading into the city. So, it was also goodbye to a quiet scenic morning, and hello to a swarm of scurrying impatient drivers.

Towards the urban surrounds of Saint-Sébastien-sur-Loire, I took the opportunity to look for a supermarket. What I actually found was a giant hypermarket just a few kilometres away - who needs super when you can have hyper?

It was only a slight detour, so I referred to Google Maps with the thought of a new coffee dripper driving me. But, having locked Terence safely outside, when I got there to look around, as hyper as this particular hypermarket was (and it was hyper, if not mega), I couldn't find one.

The few bits of food I eventually left with hadn't even warranted anything larger than a mini-market. In addition, I didn't even think about getting any lunch, which may or may not be a mistake based on my recent efforts.

On setting off from the large shopping complex, I made the rookie mistake of not restarting my bike computer to track my ride, so the next 20km of my day wasn't recorded, as I made my way south out of the sprawling city outskirts towards Le Bignon. It's always frustrating when you do that. It's proof you did the ride, right? 'If it's not on Strava, did it really happen?' But, there was not a cat's chance in hell of me going back, just to get the proof.

The busy roads led to greenery, and I was back on small country roads and lanes once again, heading towards La Roche Sur Yon. As the afternoon wore on, the problem was, as was fast becoming the theme for this ride, I had yet to pass another shop or restaurant just when I needed some lunch. So I stopped by a field to eat some of my stash of biscuits, recently procured from the Hypermarket as a snack, and cursed myself for not stocking up on baguettes.

It was two o'clock, and I still needed to book a hotel. I had sent messages to two possible hostelries earlier in the day asking if they had secure space for a bike, but I had not received a reply from either. Bugger this, I was feeling brave, so I decided to phone one.

A man answered to welcome me with a standard phrase (I assume. I had no idea what he said), and in the best French I could muster, I said, 'Bonjour. Excusez-moi. Parlez vous Anglaise?' Then I smugly waited for the positive response, bearing in mind they would no doubt be able to tell I was at least trying to speak some French.

'Non. Au Revoir'. The phone went dead.

Wow. I can only guess he has a cousin who works in a bistro in Châteaubriant that doesn't serve food.

Beginning to wonder if I should wait for a message back, I gambled and booked the other choice of hotel, another IBIS, north of La Roche Sur Yon, just off a large dual carriageway - no doubt an ideal travellers' stop.

Despite the lack of calorie intake, the rest of the afternoon went smoothly, and thanks to the Gods Of Cycling, the 1,000 extra metres of climbing didn't materialise in the end.

Towards the end of my day of cycling, and with the end in sight, I found myself motoring along at some speed for a few kilometres down a small road parallel to the main D763 road, running through a heavy industrial area, the wind pushing me along as I excitedly counted down the remaining distance.

Then I saw it: the hotel.

This part of my day would soon become one of my favourite sights. But there wasn't just one IBIS hotel; there were two, right next to each other. One looked okay, a bit like the hotel I had stayed in the night before, an IBIS Styles hotel. The other looked like an open prison - the IBIS Budget Hotel. You can probably guess which one I had booked.

The young lady was lovely at the reception desk. I say reception desk. It was more of a table at the edge of the breakfast canteen area, right inside the front door and opposite three vending machines that passed as the hotel shop. I told her I had a booking and explained that I had a bike. Luckily, she spoke English well enough, so I didn't have to resort to Google Translate. Her parentage was obviously very different from my previous encounters with French people - she was friendly and positive and said 'Oui' a lot.

I told her how good her English was, and her face lit up. I'll bank that compliment, I thought; it may come in handy.

She was slightly confused about what to do with Terence, so I told her I could take him to my room if needed. 'Oui!' she said once again and gave me a triple room near the front door to make things easier.

The room was very basic, living up to its 'budget' name with a simple but effective passion, but it did the job. It had a bed, a toilet, and a shower. There was no restaurant, but I was told I could use the restaurant in the more upmarket IBIS Styles Hotel next door. So I did.

I was starving after very little food since breakfast, so I quickly showered, changed, and headed across the car park to the fancy la-de-da IBIS.

Being in France as a 53-year-old English man who likes an early night has its perks. It was only 7pm, and there were very few patrons in the restaurant as I entered.

I was shown to a table and asked if I would like to see the menu, expecting a well-worn laminated sheet to be handed to me. But this is France, and even though it was a roadside hotel restaurant, they seemed to have a different menu every day. Ah, a small sheet of paper, perhaps?

Nope. They had two large, cumbersome A-boards with the menu written on them in chalk. My petite waitress scraped one across the floor towards my small table, making a sound like fingernails across a chalkboard, setting it up right next to me, then headed off to attend to some new arrivals. Looking down the list of food choices, I instantly recognised salad as a starter and steak as a main course. Job done. Let's keep it simple.

After the waitress returned and took my order, she grabbed the large menu and dragged it over to the new table of diners, scraping it loudly once again across the floor. Every time people walked in and settled at a table, it continued like a culinary game of drafts. A smarter server may have put any new customer right next to someone who had just ordered. Nope. They were going here, there and everywhere. With the constant dragging across the floor, I can only assume the A-board's legs erode just as quickly as the chalk they use to write the menu with. In fact, I imagine that even as we speak, someone in that restaurant is choosing their meal, looking at a menu that is, by now, in line with their shins.

But I was finally eating my first decent meal since leaving England. It tasted amazing and I felt full as I washed my two-course meal down with a couple of large glasses of beer. As my continental cousins continued arriving at the restaurant, I was ready for bed by 9 o'clock.

After four days of continuous cycling, my legs were starting to feel the strain. I had to grab and push hard on the table as I stood up, my upper leg muscles making themselves known with a stiff pain. I tried my hardest not to look eighty as I slowly rose, not grunt involuntarily, and most importantly, not topple the table. Luckily, a couple had just taken the table next to me, and there was an A-board for me to lean on and balance the load as I stood up.

I crossed the courtyard to my cell block and retired, feeling the need for deep sleep to recharge. As luck would have it, someone had checked into the hotel with a dog a few doors down and obviously left it in the room while they went off to read a hefty chalkboard. It liked to bark... And bark. My silicone earplugs went in, and I was out like a light.

102km for the day - 368m travelled.

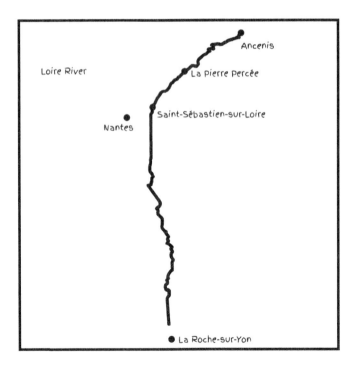

Day 5 - La Roche Sur Yon to Rochefort

'Listen very carefully, I shall say zis only once!'

After leaving my cell to join the other inmates for a budget breakfast, once again pilfering some baguettes for lunch, I decided to leave the hotel as early as possible and was on the road by 8am after treating Terence to a little TLC. Compared to the last two days of cycling, this would be a more leisurely day, relatively flat after the first 30km and only a total of 80km to La Rochelle, a popular tourist city with a rich and varied history, sitting proudly on the Atlantic coastline.

Back at home, when I was planning this ride, La Rochelle was the first place I had aimed for as I set my route. So, it felt like I was approaching the first official milestone of my journey. That said, each day seemed like a huge milestone the further I travelled from home.

The morning air was cool, and my jacket was, once again, firmly zipped up to the top. My cycling shorts hadn't even come out of the bag yet; I was still wearing trousers and two pairs of socks to keep the warmth in. My hotel, which was positioned to service the nearby commercial hub and the travellers on the main road, meant that the first few kilometres south into La Roche-Sur-Yon were heavily industrial as I continued down the small road parallel to the main D763. Before long, industry turned to commerce, and I found myself entering a large car park, serving an even larger out-of-town retail park - the Centre commercial Les Flâneries. Like the know-it-all I am, I ignored the route on my computer, second-guessing the twists and turns to cut across the vast parking areas. It didn't work, and I soon found my way blocked by a hedge and had to cycle back to the road and do firmly as I was told.

When I reached the town, La Roche-Sur-Yon looked like a nice place. Being rush hour, the traffic on the roads was busy and in a rush, so I stopped for a short while to catch my breath. I drank some water from my bottle and sat staring at a large statue of Napoleon on horseback. Doing some digging later in the day, I discovered that Napoleon had effectively created the town as it is today as a 'new town' in 1804, which once bore his name - Napoléonville. Hence, the town has a statue of him on horseback.

Then we were back on the road, dodging Citroens to get out of the town as quickly as possible.

Safely out the other side of the town, I was on rolling hills towards Lucon, with its manicured tree-lined main street that made me realise what a bit of civic pride can offer a travelling guest passing through.

A supermarket appeared, and I didn't need to be asked twice about stopping; my Sunday fun still somewhat ringing alarm bells every time I saw a shop. I stocked up on a few rations to keep me going through the day, once again enjoying the funny looks of being a man walking through a shop with a helmet on. Then, it was back on the bike. The roads were excellent, the weather was warming, and the wind gently guided me forward. The jacket even came off.

Despite the roads being large and busy, the hard shoulders to the side were perfect for bikes and I chugged along nicely, taking full advantage of the gusts of wind from passing lorries. Just after lunchtime, I had already arrived at the edge of La Rochelle.

When you see glamorous photos online of tourist destinations, neatly cropped and filtered, it's easy to forget that you have to pass through the generically dull outskirts of a town or city to get to the money shots. Past the fast food outlets, retail parks and housing estates I cycled, this could have been any town in western Europe.

Then, I arrived at the central tourist-laden area by the sheltered harbour. It was stunning.

It was also hectic, with parents trying to hold back excited children from the water's edge and couples romantically strolling along the harbour walkway. My thoughts of enjoying a nice, quiet lunch in a restaurant had been a pipe dream, and not for the last time on my trip I felt completely out of place pushing Terence along - an inconvenience to the day-trippers taking their thousands of photos.

Of course, even I can't begrudge them that. Except, of course, one such variation - the so-called 'influencer'. I've seen this species more and more over the past few years at tourist spots. There's me, just wanting a quick selfie at one of the famous views of The Colosseum to prove that I've been there, or very memorably by the Rosary Quay in Bruges, and you can't get a look in because there's a line of these idiots, acting like film stars, with their photographer buddies taking endless shots without a care in the world, or any appreciation that there are hundreds of people waiting.

I once sat in a pub garden in Basingstoke with my girlfriend as we watched one such ridiculous scene. I say watched; it was more of a gawp. Like David Attenborough, the first time he sees a new species of animal in the wild. A young woman sat fiddling with camera setups and a tripod, trying different angles and taking hundreds of test shots as her boyfriend sat romantically staring at his phone on the other side of the table. When their food came, it was action time. She positioned plates and un-drunk drinks on the table and bossed him around on how to sit. Then, for the next ten minutes, she must have taken a million photos (approximately) while their food just sat there. When she was finally happy (will she ever truly be?), the young man went back to his phone, absently picking at his fries, and she diverted her attention to her phone to check her bounty. I don't think they strung a single sentence together with each other the whole time, but I'm sure the caption to the posted photo said something very different. Who says romance is dead?

As I wandered lonely as a cloud through throngs of people around the dock, ruing my lost opportunity to be a tourist, I felt the need for some space. I walked across the quay, past the boats to the other side of the imposing Tour de la Chaîne (Chain Tower) that guards the entrance to the harbour.

It was much quieter, and I sat down to stare at the vista, looking inward towards the towers, to eat some biscuits for lunch. It was only two o'clock, and I still hadn't booked anywhere to stay. Sticking with my now fancy habit of choosing hotels over campsites, I made yet another spontaneous decision.

I had intended to stay at La Rochelle. So I could find somewhere to stay, check in, come back to the port and be the tourist I wanted to be. Instead, I booked a hotel in Rochefort, a city 37km further south. It was Tuesday, and tomorrow I had planned to meet Ian, my friend from England (he of the sniper's tale), near the town of Cognac. If I pushed on through today, I could wipe off some distance for tomorrow and get to Cognac earlier in the day. The weather was good, and I still had a good two to three hours of cycling in me following a less-than-taxing morning. So off I went.

Possibly a bit too hastily, though. After 1.5km, having gone to take a sip from my water bottle and realising it wasn't there, I had to retrace my route to retrieve it from on top of the wall where I'd left it. That short trip back into the strong breeze made me realise how much I had benefited from a tailwind all morning.

Having extended my final destination, I was now relying on Google Maps for the rest of the day, which directed me straight to a lovely coastal walkway. The first few kilometres were beautiful. I had the path to myself, with the sea for company to my right, and I was happy bumbling along past the empty, stony beaches and the rocky outcrops.

But, as was starting to become the way with Google Maps, the fun soon began. I say fun; perhaps calamity is a better word. As I approached the edge of an abandoned beach bar, the path suddenly disappeared. It was on the map, just not in front of me. Should I go back a few kilometres and head inland?

Being that man some might refer to as stubborn (or stupid), I did the sensible thing, once again, and decided to keep moving forward. I mustered my inner Geoff Capes and lifted Terence carefully over the large rocks that began where the path abruptly ended, praying that my ankles stayed sturdy.

Slowly, guiding the bike towards the front area of the bar that had at one time been the terrace, I secretly hoped that just around the corner I would see the other end of the severed path. If the route continued like this, even for a few hundred metres, I'd be here for quite some time, lugging Terence a few steps at a time. Luckily, the terrace itself was smooth concrete, clear of rocks, so I placed Terence back on the ground and rolled him across the frontage. Then, as we rounded the corner on the other side, thankfully, the trail reappeared.

The path on the other side of the bar soon led to a country lane, which, in turn, fed me out onto a larger road and before long, the coast was well and truly behind me. I powered on towards my destination, at one point cycling parallel to a busy highway, with the wind twisting around me and the constant whirr of passing cars on loud concrete dominating my eardrums.

I was starting to feel a little tired, and began yawning approximately every ten seconds, as I rode on, counting down the kilometres, but feeling very smug with the extra distance I was putting in. This was going to end up being a mammoth day of cycling.

Eventually, I arrived at Rochefort and started heading for my hotel. I rambled past the retail parks and meandered through the back streets before appearing in the centre ville, with its wide boulevards and luscious green squares. I had cycled just short of 130 kilometres and been in the saddle for over seven hours.

The hotel I had booked was a boutique, independent hotel, and the petite young lady who welcomed me certainly made it feel like it. With my social reference points firmly stuck in the past, she reminded me of Mimi Labonq, the short blond waitress in Alo Alo, but much less raunchy, and much more innocent. She looked confused when I said, complete with a thick French accent, 'Listen very carefully; I shall say this only once!'

I didn't, of course, I just thought it. But we navigated the check-in routine, and she was able to put in much more effort than I could on the translation front as we stumbled our way through the paperwork process. I felt like I was one of the first real-life English people she'd ever met in Rochefort.

'You speak very good English', I said as she coyly giggled and carried on checking me in. I hoped she understood this wasn't my clumsy way of flirting - after all, I'm no René Artois. It was simply my ongoing ploy of making her do all the language heavy lifting.

Terence was offered a garage in which to rest overnight, and I hoofed the two rear pannier bags with my clothes in up to my room. By now, my bag routine was beginning to take shape - what went where and how to pack things efficiently for balance. Packing cubes had made my life so much easier on that front, so I guess I had stupid adverts on Instagram to thank for something.

Showered and feeling a little fresher, I unzipped my 'tee shirts and stretching' packing cube and did my stretches on the bed to make sure my legs didn't seize up. I was still getting aches and pains and finding it a fun challenge to walk downstairs without looking like a puppet on strings. My personal favourite circumstance in terms of stiffness issues had fast become when I went to stand up after prolonged sessions of sitting down, which, of course, invariably only happened in crowded restaurants and buffet breakfast rooms, as if an audience was essential.

I had a specific reason for visiting Rochefort and would treat myself in the morning, but for now, it was time to head out for something to eat. My new

French friend fluttered her eyelashes as she put crosses on a map of the town and showed me where the restaurants were. Once again, the young lady's cheeks reddened as I complimented her grasp of the English language.

Being centrally placed in the town, I turned left at the end of Avenue Lafayette and stumbled across the entrance to the Arsenal de Rochefort, an old French naval base and dockyard, which had been operational for 250 years since 1665, closing in 1926. It had a couple of ships in the dry docks, but as tourist attractions go, it wasn't jaw-dropping. That said, the only reason I wanted my jaw to drop right now was to stuff some food into my mouth, so I carried on wandering back into the town.

I found myself in a large square with two busy bistros on opposite sides. Still confused on etiquette, I wasn't quite sure what I was meant to do - just sit at a table and wait for service or go inside. So I bottled it and carried on wandering. I passed a few small bars with men drinking coffee and chatting outside, wondering if I would ever find somewhere sensible to eat that I could cope with.

An imposing Italian restaurant passed me by. I stopped, checked my map and looked for the crosses. I remember Mimi mentioning an Italian restaurant, and as luck would have it I had stumbled right upon it.

I swallowed hard and went inside, not quite knowing what to expect. It was three-quarters full and bustling with busy waitresses, one of whom welcomed me in fast-flowing French. 'Une table pour une s'il vous plaît' - it was my turn to be coy. Two minutes later, I was supping a beer and using a translation app on my phone to work out what was on the menu.

As much as I love Italian food, I feel that when I am in a foreign country, I should really try to stick to local foods. But food was food at this point, so I'll save that thought for a day when I've not cycled 130km. Besides, who doesn't love Italian?

The owner came over to take my order, an Italian matriarch who looked like she didn't take shit from anybody. I awkwardly ordered a large calamari starter and a chicken risotto, which was more challenging than it sounds, as she slipped casually between French and Italian during every other sentence. Maman Mia!

With hindsight, I should have paid closer attention to the translation app. My starter was lovely, but the Risotto contained curry powder and tasted like a weak, creamy chicken curry. But, I was fed, watered and content.

I made sure my audience was ready as I stood up from the table with my now customary grunting, legs straining. They enjoyed it, not so much by clapping and cheering, but through sniggering and whispering.

Rather than provide an encore, and full up on pasta and bread, I waddled out of the restaurant and slowly back to the hotel.

I finished my non-French evening by watching Arsenal beat Chelsea 5-0 on my computer. It had been a very rewarding day all round.

129.5km for the day - 497.5km travelled.

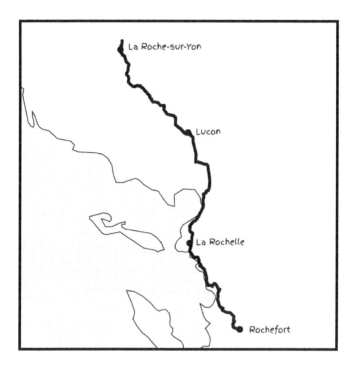

Day 6 - Rochefort to Roissac

'Who'd of thought a couple of grunts like us from Basingstoke would ever be here experiencing this?'

After yesterday's additional exertion, today would only involve 80km of cycling, and I had a specific destination and some social activity to look forward to this evening.

My friend Ian was flying out from the UK, and I had planned to meet him later at the home of a friend of his living in France, just south of the town of Cognac; another Ian, just to confuse things.

When I came downstairs from my hotel room, my lovely little French receptionist was in the lounge serving breakfast. It always amazes me in hotels when I see the same person from late the night before there greeting me early the following morning. It must be a hard job and I have a lot of respect for people who choose to do it.

Judging by her skin, My over-active age-o-meter guessed Mimi to be in her twenties. But, despite her youthful demeanour, she had the posture and personality of a fifty-year-old - a Mrs Overall in training. I could imagine her now welcoming patrons well into her nineties, regaling them with stories about the time she met a strange English man, travelling on a bike, who grunted every time he stood up.

Characters like her make places for me, whether it's a bar, restaurant or hotel, and she was the perfect pocket-sized host. So much so, in fact, I didn't even steal any breakfast rolls that morning, although I may well have sneaked out a pastry.

I've stayed in hotels of all shapes and sizes, and it's always the smaller ones you remember. For example, in the late summer of 2020, I had a very memorable stay at a small family hotel in Pembrokeshire. Covid rules at the time meant that if you were in public spaces indoors, unless you were sitting down, you still had to wear a face mask. The virus had developed a sincere sense of etiquette by then.

I still remember the husband and wife team so clearly, especially at breakfast time, when it would take the man, perhaps too old to be working, at least five minutes to bring any one thing from the kitchen. It wasn't ideal, especially as he could only carry a couple of things at once. God help you if he forgot the HP sauce on his first trip. Rather than simply cleaning the tables between guests, he had developed a system where he assigned each group a specific table on arrival. He'd not quite perfected his plan, though; he spent half the time moving tables around when people turned up so there was sufficient distance between groups, which, considering his speed, wasn't a quick process. By the time we'd finished breakfast each day, it was time for bed.

Thinking about it, perhaps he learned the technique watching waitresses move a menu board at a roadside hotel restaurant in Northern France.

Having finished my breakfast, I said my au revoirs to Mimi and recovered Terence from the hotel garage, loading him up with more organisational skill than ever, before setting off down the hill to my first stop.

The morning sky was dim and damp and threatening to rain as I headed south towards the River Charente to see if it lived up to its 16th-century billing from King Francis I of 'the most beautiful river in the kingdom'.

I had a date with the last operational transporter bridge in France. I was doubly glad to discover it was operational, because the road bridge downriver was imposingly massive, and I didn't fancy my chances of getting over it.

Built in 1900, the Rochefort-Martrou Transporter Bridge is a tall steel framework spanning the river - it has to be high to let the boats through - with a moving gondola platform hanging from the frame at land level that acts as the crossing. Operated as a working bridge until 1967, it is now a Listed Historical Monument in France and a tourist crossing for passengers on foot, or, luckily for me this morning, a bike. With a small bit of English pride, by the way, it's worth noting that the world's longest transporter bridge is in Middlesbrough, crossing the River Tees. In true English style, it's not actually working at the moment.

The journey across the river lasted less than ninety seconds. I was joined on the large, slippery platform by a young family and, I am guessing, a grandfather proudly showing his grandson how things used to be. There was a lot of childlike excitement, mainly from the grandfather.

Then, as quickly as it started, it was time to get off at the other side into the small village of Échillais.

The rest of my morning consisted of quiet country roads interspersed with cycle paths similar to bridleways. The sky was beginning to brighten, and all the while the terrain stayed firm and the paths relatively smooth I was fine with being off-road. Then it was back on the small country roads, cycling through lovely villages and some quintessentially French lanes lined with trees - the sort you've seen in every movie ever set in the French countryside.

I was really enjoying the day and I had plenty of time on my side.

Around lunchtime, my phone pinged. It was a message from my friend Ian. He'd landed in France, picked up his hire bike and was on his way to meet his friend for the 110km drive to Cognac. The world was good and the day was running smoothly.

About half an hour later, my phone pinged again. 'I've busted the bike! Front wheel nut has sheared off the axle. Heading back to the bike shop to get it mended. Will update you in an hour. My phone is on 2%!'

Oh dear, that sounded fun.

I couldn't do anything but carry on towards Saintes. A small city with the most beautiful river in the kingdom running through the middle, this was the first daytime stop I'd taken on my journey that had any signs of life, and it was the perfect place to grab some lunch.

I duly cycled toward the centre ville to look for somewhere suitable to stop, pushing Terence down into the old town and settling in at a small café for a panini. I was once again an oddity, but I was getting used to people staring at me. I can't speak for Terence, though; he was also getting some looks. I think his were for all the right reasons of being cool, though, rather than looking like a pasty buffoon.

As I waited for my food to arrive, I did some Googling to find out more about Saintes, which had some form in the history books as the first Roman capital of Aquitaine.

Cycling down to the river after lunch, I popped by The Arch of Germanicus to take a quick peek. It had originally stood over the terminus of the Roman road from Lyon to Saintes and dates back to approximately 18AD. Duly impressed, both with the history and the fact that I took the time to look, I popped to the public toilet next to the Tourist office nearby. Even that had old Roman Pillars standing guard.

The afternoon of cycling was mainly fast, flat and straight, all the way to Cognac, 12km north of my final destination; the small village of Roissac.

The landscape could have been more inspiring, and my main point of interest for the afternoon was the lack of fencing next to the railway lines that ran parallel to the road I was on.

As I reached a road junction at Chaniers, I was struck by how very rudimentary the railway crossing was. No full-height gates sweeping down or flashing lights that could illuminate Wembley to warn pedestrians and motorists like you'd get in England. There were just a couple of large sticks painted red that come down halfway across the road. It's as if French people don't need to be told that going on a train track is a silly idea. No need for fences or warning signs here, just an ounce (or gram) of common sense.

This is where we truly differ from our French cousins. In the UK, if someone was injured on a train line, it would be blamed on the train company for not having enough signs or fences, and law firms would get involved faster than a TGV. In France, they'd just shrug and mumble, 'un idiot!'.

I wasn't sure what to expect from Cognac, and I entered the town on a small road with an unassuming sign welcoming me. I'd still not heard back from Ian about his broken bike, and it was now around three o'clock. I headed towards the castle, which sat beside the pretty river I had crossed twice today - the Charente. There wasn't much to see, so I sat by the water for a while before deciding to go for a drink, while I waited to hear.

Google Maps set me off into the town, and I visited three closed bars before finding one open by a busy roundabout. It was time for a beer and some admin as I waited to hear from Ian.

Still no news after an hour, I took a chance and carried on cycling, assuming that he must be on his way as it was only an hour or so drive from Bordeaux.

For some reason, I expected this last bit of my day to be a short ride, but I still had 11km to go, and it would end up being the hilliest part of the day.

Knowing I was being treated to dinner and put up for the night, it would be rude to arrive empty-handed, so I piled more weight on to Terence with a nice bottle of red wine (apparently, in France, all wine is excellent), and some beer from a small shop, then headed south out of Cognac.

The rest of the day's cycling was into the wind to add a little extra challenge. Over the last few kilometres of rolling countryside, I was surrounded by vineyards on the left and a large military airbase on the right before rising up into the village, arriving forty or so minutes later, ready to look for the address I'd been given.

Despite being a tiny village, I couldn't find the house anywhere. I found the street but could not find the number. So I perched myself next to the Fontaines De Roissac - a row of concrete troughs that seemed overkill for such a small hamlet - and waited. Our host told me later that a local dignitary had gifted them to the villagers many years ago after they had helped his injured wife. Right now, they were perfect for sitting on and drinking one of the beers I'd bought for my host.

I didn't have much of a signal on my phone where I was and had still not heard from Ian, so I just waited and hoped I was in the right place.

After about twenty minutes of sitting, waiting and stretching, a small car pootled around the corner. I didn't recognise the driver, but luckily, I did recognise the passenger, despite the fact that he had a small dog on his lap.

I was soon to get to know the driver, though - Ian (yes, another one, let's call him French Ian), our very generous host for the night.

The weather was pleasant, and I followed the car fifty yards to the house, where I parked Terence and said proper hellos. We sat in Ian's beautiful floral garden while he popped in and out of the house, bringing back cold beers, wine, and the most amazing bread and cheese. I would have been happy with that as a meal, but this was just the pre-starter starter.

The cheese was flavoursome, the bread was fresh and crusty, and the beer tasted sweet. I was transported into a scene from a light French romantic comedy as my friend Ian told me the story of his day's journey. (Obviously, he was the comic sidekick in my movie, with me being the hero who gets the girl.)

Following his damaged bike debacle (a damage he himself had caused trying to remove the wheel), he had returned to the bike shop to get it repaired. Then, after hooking up with French Ian, they had been off the grid all afternoon, enjoying a guided tour of the local area, including a visit to a Pineau distillery and a trout farm.

Pineau, or, to give it its full name, Pineau des Charentes, is a regional aperitif made from fortified wine and Cognac eau-de-vie. It turns out that my friend Ian had been sampling the wares, fully encouraged by French Ian. This meant that he was already a few drinks ahead of me, which, in real terms, using a handicap system based on my experience drinking with him, equalled us out at this stage.

French Ian was putting us both up in a friend's converted barn for the night, which added to the film adaptation running around my head as we strolled up to the beautiful building with our bikes, just as the lowering sun was starting to drain the heat from the day.

We put away our bits, and I had a speedy and cold shower (French Ian was mortified when it dawned on him during the walk over that he'd forgotten to turn on the hot water earlier in the day). Trying to warm up in my room afterwards, I stood by the large bedroom window in the warm rays of the fading sun, towel around my waist, looking out over to the vineyards on the horizon. I patiently waited for

Vanessa Paradis to turn up as the pretty local girl who had been waiting all her life for a greying, chubby stranger to cycle into the dull village and whisk her off her feet. She never arrived, and I soon snapped out of it as Ian brought me back to reality, shouting from the next room, 'Are you ready yet, Killick?'.

What can I say about the rest of the evening? It was exceptional and will no doubt stay with me as one of those few lifetime memories we are lucky to have once in a while.

Sometimes, you just have to sit back and pinch yourself, asking, 'How lucky am I?'. I pondered on the chain of events that brought me (a scrote from Basingstoke) to this part of the world, with these people in this environment, something I discovered that my old friend with me from Basingstoke was also thinking.

We were joined during the evening by Mico, a French/Australian friend of (French) Ian's, and the owner and distiller of a gin brand called Audemus. The four of us shared stories from our lives, as Mico poured the perfect Pink Pepper G&T, garnished with Rosemary from the very bush that was part of the original story of Audemus.

Vanessa Paradis still hadn't turned up, but my male companions would do.

Cognac and Pineau were both offered as an aperitif. When in Rome, I thought. I gave them a go, but they are not my bag at all, and a sip is all I managed.

Luckily, my English cycling buddy managed to take up the slack and finish mine off.

The fresh trout on offer, something I would not usually eat (especially with it making those eyes at me on the plate), was absolutely delicious, and never have I had such a simple-looking meal with so much flavour.

On a 22-day cycle ride bursting with new memories, mulling over this experience a few weeks later in the cold light of day, although the day of riding itself was nothing special, the evening, the setting, the company, and the generosity of a stranger will stay with me forever.

83km for the day - 580.5km travelled.

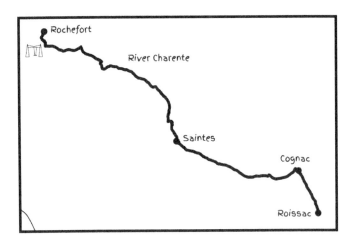

Day 7 - Roissac to Bordeaux

'Hey mate, there's a little bit of a problem. It turns out I didn't actually book a room.'

Continuing the storyline of my French romantic comedy, I woke up in a sleepy haze, rolled out of bed and hobbled towards the window, my legs stiff and unwilling to cooperate. I dramatically opened both curtains to reveal the beautiful French countryside and silence. I say silence; Ian was in the room next door and had decided to make an early morning phone call.

In front of me, topped with terracotta roof tiles, a stone wall about head height surrounded the loosely manicured lawn down to the gate and a gravel driveway. An early blooming Wisteria stretched across the wall, merging with short-cut hedges surrounding some built-in storage cupboards. Behind a small line of trees beyond the wall, rolling hills held regimented columns of vines - thousands of them. A beautifully romantic scene for a boy from Basingstoke, despite learning about the aggressive farming techniques of the wine growers the night before.

Taking advantage of the shower facilities once again, which were now pumping out steaming hot water, I slowly prepared for another day of cycling.

Packing my kit had become a much more organised affair by now, and I felt I'd finally developed a system that worked for the constant packing and unpacking each day. Then I headed down the stairs that ran down the side of the barn, leaning to the right against the wall with my arm, my legs still not quite playing ball in the 'going down stairs' department.

Ian was waiting for me, preparing his bike. We grunted our good mornings, finished loading our bikes and rolled away from our overnight haven towards French Ian's house for breakfast.

As we opened the door to the kitchen, there was an instant smell of brewing coffee and fresh bread. There really is no finer smell in the world, especially first thing in the morning and especially after an evening of G&Ts. Our genial host had, once again, pulled out all of the stops with fresh orange juice, warm croissants with butter and cassis accompaniments, and two crusty baguettes fresh from the oven.

I liberally covered a piece of fresh bread with the best goat's cheese I'd ever tasted and sipped on a strong coffee. If Carling did overnight stays in a stereotypical French Village with dinner and breakfast, they would be hard-pushed to beat this one, with or without Vanessa Paradis as a romantic love interest.

After another carb-loaded breakfast, we said our goodbyes and thank yous with solid hugs. It just didn't feel enough as we slowly sauntered off, leaving French Ian with a table to clear and, I hope, the satisfaction of creating memories for two very contented men.

The coffee had done its job, but we were both feeling the effects of a late night and, perhaps, one G&T too many. It was an evening that would stay in my memory for a long time, if not forever, so I was okay with the payoff as I tried to cycle off the fug.

The morning's ride was very much up and down, cycling through the rolling hills of wine country. Ian spent the morning regaling me with various facts that he'd learned the day before on his car journey, and we very slowly warmed up to the day's challenge.

'So that thing there… in the middle of the field… is a massive gas heater. When it's cold or frosty, they light it up, and it billows warm air across the field. That huge fan next to it blows it all around. Awful when you think about it.'

'And sometimes, they even use helicopters just to push warm air down into the fields.'

I let him have his moment despite the fact we'd gone through all this last night.

I had planned our first coffee stop of the morning in Jonzac, the town I had targeted initially as my overnight stop before I had had the fortune of being offered the evening I'd just had.

26km into the day, and many, many more facts about France later, I knew the town was close but hadn't been taking much notice of the route as we cycled along. I was starting to wonder why the town hadn't appeared yet and why road signs to Jonzac were pointing to the right rather than straight ahead. I stopped to check our position. We were 2km east of the town, and it was behind us. Oops.

Despite both looking like we needed another hit of caffeine or two, we decided to continue.

Ian did a sterling job of slowing down for me on every upward slope, reassuring me that my slow pace was good for him, and we continued nibbling away at the day's distance.

At 48km into our journey, I could see the town of Montendre ahead on the map. We decided to stop there and grab some lunch to fuel us for the afternoon. We'd still have 60km to go, but the day was starting to drag out.

It was great to have company, but I found the going hard as the landscape rolled along. The constant up and down was hitting my legs on what would end up being the day with the most climbing I'd had on the trip so far. Yes, it was lumpy.

It was a relief as we hit Montendre. I could stop, eat, drink and rest, ready for the push to Bordeaux.

As we entered the town on a long flat road, there was a large supermarket on the left with a restaurant adjoined. We didn't want that, though; we wanted traditional French fare. So we trudged up a steep hill into the town centre to search for a bistro.

As we weaved in and out of the market traders packing away for the day, catching our breath after the sharp ascent, we just couldn't find one. It was proof, if needed, of the situation I found myself in so many times on the journey so far, and Ian was, unfortunately for him, on the end of my daily whinge. With a witness in play, I doubled down. I'm not sure he was too chuffed, but I felt better for having an audience to moan to.

I consulted Google, which offered two restaurants a little further down the road towards the other side of the town. The first one didn't exist; it was just a row of houses. The other, Restaurant Cave La Quincaillerie, looked rather posh. It also looked rather closed.

Fortunately, Ian speaks French very well, having lived in southern France in his younger days helping English families on their camping holidays (and much, much more, having often listened to stories from his youth). He popped his head inside the door of the restaurant to see if they were taking patrons for lunch, and I could see him look upwards as he stepped half inside. The restaurant was upstairs, and the answer was, thankfully, Oui. We could go in, even though we were dressed like two extras from The Village People.

I locked Terence up with Ian's nameless hire bike, and we (me) slowly walked up the stairs. I'd become accustomed to using the handrail at every opportunity by now.

Small, smart tables ran around an expansive balcony, with a full-length window covering the front of the building looking out over the town. The place was empty, and we were led to a small table for two down one side of the balcony. Menus were offered as we sat down, with me taking twice as long as Ian to achieve this simple feat.

There was no chance of getting a burger and frites in here; it was local artisan food with a menu that looked like it changed regularly depending on the season.

I asked for a Coke and was given a sarcastic French scoff in return. Of course, silly me, their only soft drinks were local juices and fizzy, flavoured waters. So, I joined Ian's artisan train and had a local blonde beer instead.

Through a lack of options, while searching for an eatery in the town, we had stumbled upon a restaurant with a nationwide accolade for local gastronomy - the Master Restaurateur in Montendre.

By the time our starters came, the place was packed with older, affluent-looking couples dining and what looked like a large, important business lunch taking place on the large table by the front window. Each new patron took a double take when they saw us with our shorts and cycling gear as they appeared at the top of the wide stairway that led into the restaurant.

The food was excellent, but it was not something I fully appreciated at the time. I just wanted bulky food, and I wanted it speedily so that we could crack on with our day. It was neither.

As a local, artisan restaurant, of course, they stocked Audemus Gin, and my excited companion took the chance to explain to the waiter how he had designed the packaging and the website, and that only last night we had dined with the owner of the drinks brand. The waiter looked bemused as Ian took out his phone to show him his website as proof. Ian, on the other hand, was convinced that the waiter had seemed incredibly interested in what he'd had to say after he'd coyly moved away to wait on the other patrons.

'Is that really what you took from that little interaction?' I replied. 'Interesting.'

When the waiter returned, he was much more chatty, though, so Ian's charm offensive must have worked, once again proving I'm just an old cynic.

As much as we wanted to hurry, they were busy in the restaurant, and it wasn't the kind of place that rushed its dinner service. It was over an hour later before I grabbed the handrail tight and made my way daintily down the staircase and back out to unlock the bikes, full after two courses of rich game. Ian was still chatting with the waiter after seeing his beloved pop-up display for the gin brand on the reception desk counter, busy explaining its design. To be fair, the Frenchman's nonchalant-o-meter had cooled, and he was at least nodding.

It was still cold and grey, and rain was starting to float in and out of our afternoon as we continued south. The green countryside slowly faded away as the kilometres passed, becoming more urban the closer we got to Bordeaux.

Once again, I was caught by surprise as we arrived at the crossing of The Dordogne. I found the rivers exciting points of reference on this trip. I had heard their names so many times in films and on TV but didn't exactly know where these waterways were in the geography of France.

As we headed towards the bridge over the wide crossing, we found ourselves tucked onto a small pathway off the road to the right. Rather than staying on the road and holding up the traffic - it was a pretty long bridge - we had veered off for a safer crossing.

The only issue was that when the pathway itself hit the bridge, it got incredibly narrow, something I nearly missed at the time. I was too busy trying to video the sign by the side of the road announcing the river.

Cycling one-handed, with a kerb the size of what seemed like a single-storey building inches to my left, I quickly focused on the more critical endeavour of staying alive. The camera went away fast, and I focused my eyes on the end of the bridge, hanging on for dear life as I wobbled along the narrow strip of concrete, trying my very best to stay as upright as possible.

Ian was in front of me by about twenty metres, doing the same thing until, about halfway across, he suddenly stopped and got off his bike. With no traffic coming from either direction, I watched in bemusement as he lifted his bike across the road.

I looked over to see a lovely wide, segregated cycle path running on the other side of the bridge. I'm not quite sure how we'd missed it on the run-in.

I went to follow suit, Terence being somewhat heavier than his sleek gravel bike, and we both heaved the load through a gap in the crossed struts of the bridge dividing the path from the road. Relieved, we stood overlooking the dark, murky water below, catching our breath, as well as each other's eye, both in wonderment at the hairy situation we'd just found ourselves in.

The weather turned dark through the surrounding towns on the outskirts of Bordeaux, and we were hit with a downpour of rain. This was made even more interesting as we came into Lormont, the damp brakes doing all they could to guide us safely over cobbled streets before descending a steep hill onto the banks of the Garonne, the wide sweeping river that runs through the centre of Bordeaux before joining the Dordogne 20km or so north and spreading its watery wings into the Atlantic.

We still had six kilometres to go to the hotel as the rain stopped as quickly as it had begun, and we followed the river southwards through flat industrial areas, the ground drying fast. As we neared the city centre, the factories and traffic were replaced by parks, with people strolling and cycling in the spring afternoon.

We eventually reached our river crossing at Pont de Pierre before entering the last kilometre of the day's ride into a busy tourist area. The 'stone bridge' had been built in the first part of the 19th century on the orders of Napoleon. The little fella sure did get around.

As we neared the hotel, I said a brief goodbye to Ian, and he went back to the hire shop to return his bike. I carried on to the hotel where Lorraine was waiting to see me. Tomorrow, I would be having a day off, and she'd taken the time to fly out and bring anything I might need. She had also had to endure a 36-hour cancellation notice on her flight out because of a strike by French Traffic Controllers, forcing her to come a day early on the same day she found out at great expense - what a gal!

I messaged her quickly to ask her to video me coming in. She was in the hotel reception, and I was full of excitement at the thought of seeing her as my route twisted off the main road. For some reason, best known to Strava, I cycled up to the hotel from the opposite direction to the one we were both expecting, and as I rounded the corner I saw her 20 yards away, camera ready, facing the other way.

'Hi', I said as I rolled in behind her. She did what she does a lot - and one of the reasons why she is my most favourite person in the world - she laughed very, very loudly. I'd missed her laughing. I'd missed her full stop.

She ordered me to go back and come round the corner again and look surprised. I did as I was told. I usually do.

Film footage sorted, we parked Terence, pride of place, next to the hire bikes in the car park of the hotel. Then, together, we lugged my bags upstairs, with me holding the bannister tightly. Going up wasn't as bad now after one week of cycling; it was just the downward travel where my quad muscles started gaining independence from my direction of travel.

The hotel room was nice - a small duplex apartment. Although it didn't particularly feel like luxury, we'd been upgraded, which came in incredibly handy twenty minutes later when I received a phone call from Ian.

'Hey mate, there's a little bit of a problem. It turns out I didn't actually book my room.'

Having just showered, sitting on the sofa with only a towel to hide my modesty, I wasn't quite ready to face the public, so Lorraine went down to help. The reception was very busy with an influx of guests, so they cheekily faded to the edges of the commotion, and Ian was duly smuggled into our apartment to use the sofa bed for the night.

After we'd both changed, we headed out for something to eat, aiming for the city's tourist area, stumbling upon a traditional-looking French restaurant on a busy road. It wasn't too cold, so we took a table outside where we chatted, ate, and drank.

After each guessing completely wrong many times, we discovered our young waiter's name was Arthur, much to our surprise. He must have felt like a sideshow when we asked, and even more so after the next round of our game, which involved guessing his age.

We didn't end up moving for the rest of the night, for which my legs were very grateful, and even after we'd paid the bill and were ready to leave, another bottle of rose was ordered, thanks to Ian, delaying my much-needed early night.

Eventually, we stumbled back to the hotel where, after clambering up the stairs to our hotel room, hand firmly on the stair rail, I did the same again in our little duplex, dawdling up to the bedroom, where I climbed across the bed in the tiny alcove and passed out immediately.

108km for the day - 688km travelled.

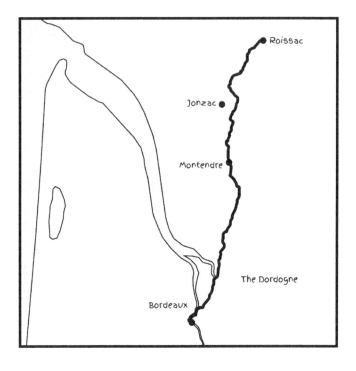

Day 8 - 'Rest' Day

'Yah, Jonty, he's put the pin in the next bar already, we have to go. Drink up!

By the time I woke up at 7:30am, a lay-in for me, Ian had already left to catch his early morning flight home. I had heard nothing, thanks to my earplugs. He does like a flying visit, does Ian.

It seemed strange not having to prepare to cycle as soon as I got up, doing my stretching, scrambling around for some breakfast, and undertaking The Krypton Factor routine of packing my bags.

By mid-morning, though, I had itchy feet. As tired as I thought I might be, and with the chance to take a rest, I really didn't want to waste a day in a foreign city with Lorraine.

So we wandered. The weather was warm enough for my coat to come off as we strolled by the river. There didn't seem to be an amazing amount worth seeing in the city that floated our boat, or maybe I wasn't in the mood. So, we ended up mooching through a flea market before settling down at a café to watch the trams go by.

We sauntered a bit more, taking a quick look around the Cathédrale Saint-André, then enjoying another 'un café' in the square. But, it has to be said, if you've seen inside one overly extravagant church jam-packed with riches, you've seen them all.

Back at the hotel, some of my clothes were introduced to the washing machine as I tinkered with Terence, tweaking gear shifts and giving him a good clean with what I had at hand.

I also examined the replacement bottom bracket that Graham, my bike guy, had sent out with Lorraine, along with all the tools to replace it. She'd not thought twice about putting them in her hand luggage on the way out, and was somewhat bemused when she got stopped at security and asked why she was carrying so many potential weapons.

Graham had been a star in sourcing a new part for Terence over the past few days, and I was tempted to take the bracket replacement and tools with me or at least change it there and then. But, after those first couple of days of worry in Northern France, the noise had disappeared, and I didn't want to risk making things worse. The clacking never did come back.

After a lazy afternoon, we took an early evening stroll down to the river, where we found a bar to have a couple of drinks. There were groups of English Rugby tourists (acting like groups of English rugby tourists), but it was only to be expected. It was music to my ears when they finally left.

'Yah, Jonty, he's put a pin in the next bar already, we have to go. Drink up! Come on, I'll hold you. Yes, this way. Mind that table of people.'

Not wanting to overreach ourselves on the alcohol front, we went off to find some food, walking a few metres back down the river to a lovely Italian restaurant - Ragazzi Da Peppone.

It was bustling inside, and the food and the atmosphere were wonderful. Plus, there was a nice little touch when it came to choosing the wine. There was no menu or large chalkboard being scraped across the floor to pick out your drink of choice. You had to go down to the wine cave, pick your own bottle from the large selection and bring it back up, holding on tightly to the handrail, of course. I left that to Lorraine.

12,000 steps that don't count - 688km travelled.

Day 9 - Bordeaux to Mimizan Plage

'The place stinks unbearably of a mixture of burnt car tyres and rotten eggs.'

The morning came far too quickly and was joined, rather instantly, by a dull headache. Even though it felt like we'd only just said bonjour, it was time to say adieu to Lorraine and continue my journey.

We both quietly packed our bags for the next leg of our travels, hers back to England and mine 94km south to a campsite on the shores of the lake Biscarrosse-Parentis. Her packing was done in about ten seconds; mine took somewhat longer, so she helped me prepare the bike for the day. Having bundled our bags down to reception, I took great pleasure getting in everyone's way when I brought the bike in.

Standing outside the front of the hotel, with bags fastened and straps tightened, our goodbyes were all rather rushed in the end when her taxi arrived early. In what seemed like slow motion, we hugged before she turned, leaned down and got into the back of the car.

As I closed the door behind her, staring through the car window, a feeling of love and gratitude swept over me as the car set off slowly, bobbling along the cobbled side street. Terence looked on a little jealous, no doubt feeling like the third wheel in the relationship, and the fourth, for that matter.

I would now have two weeks on my own before seeing her again, and although we would continue to speak most nights on video chat, it's just not the same without a nice squidgy cuddle. She continues to be such a massive source of support for me - not just for this ride but for everything - and she has brought a lot of fun to my life at a time when I thought I'd lost it forever.

Even the stress of her cancelled flight leading up to this trip became an adventure for Lorraine, which says a lot about her approach to living. While I would have undoubtedly thrown my toys out of the pram, she went headlong into making her flying visit happen, ending up having to shell out for a second expensive flight, and an extra night staying with a local artist in an Airbnb. I often wish I was more like her because, spending the time I spend with her, I have realised that it's amazing the adventures you can end up having.

With Terence packed up and neither of us raring to go, we set off. The day was going to be a flat day of cycling, ideal after having a day off, but the sky was looking dark and threatening. At least it wasn't raining as I slowly peddled away, taking my turn to bobble on the cobbles.

Despite being quite central in the city, I followed the directions from my bike computer through back streets and small squares with very little traffic. No doubt, the bistros and bars dotted around bustled in the summer evenings, but for now, they were lifeless as I made my way towards the edge of the city on this early Saturday morning.

After three kilometres of gentle cycling, my mojo still nowhere to be seen, a quick check on the bike computer made me question my direction. The distance remaining for the day that showed on the screen was much higher than I was expecting it to be. A quick stop on the side of the road enlightened me.

I had not set the hotel as the starting point on the bike computer, so it had rerouted to take me on a completely different path, around 20km longer than planned. Good start!

Using Google Maps to rejoin the original route, I crisscrossed the southern outskirts of Bordeaux. Through back streets and over footbridges I cycled, at one point weaving through a throng of eager parents chatting away in the middle of the road, and not moving an inch as they dropped their teenage children off for a school trip. Gossiping with each other seemed more interesting than their children's excitement.

Eventually, after adding a few unnecessary kilometres to my day, I was back on track and heading down the D1250 - a long, straight, 23km stretch of road heading to the town of Biganos.

Unlike The Holly's ditty, this road *was* long, with no winding turns whatsoever and was lined with what seemed a constant flow of shops, garages and houses.

As the morning wore on, with people going about their business, the stream of traffic was steady. The hard shoulder on the side of the road protected me from the cars, and protected the drivers from having to sit behind me, shuffling along at 20km per hour.

I was making good progress, and I was keen to make the most of food stops as I saw them. So I stopped for a pastry and un café in a roadside bakery. My breakfast that morning had consisted of yet another baguette, and I had learned that fuelling in the morning was essential to make the day more manageable in the afternoon. That was my excuse for a Pain Au Chocolate, anyway.

Part way down the long and tedious stretch, I reached the town of Marcheprime and decided to take a look down one of the roads for another food stop. It was like a ghost town with few houses, no shops and no cafés, just a massive school complex. Perhaps I was entering towns at completely the wrong points, but far too often, I couldn't work them out. Where were all the people? And where on earth do they eat? I got back on the D1250 and carried on.

The first part of my day had been lovely. But it soon got busier, wetter and more miserable as the road started to spread out away from Bordeaux. By the time I eventually reached Baganos, it was raining hard, and within minutes, I couldn't wait to get through the town and out the other side. The traffic was dangerous and unforgiving as I stood my ground, but I was struggling to see through the large raindrops having a party on my glasses.

Out the other side of the town, with some relief, the concrete stopped, and greenery hit once again. It had been like cycling in England, with people driving far too close for comfort to shave seconds from their trip. As much as I know cyclists can be annoying, they are still human beings. Perhaps I should have ridden a horse. It seems people slow down to almost a stop when one of those is on the road leaving large piles of shit in their wake.

As if reading my mind, the day decided to reward my trial of perilous town cycling with a sudden stop in the rain. The sun was peaking through the clouds in the distance, and I enjoyed some delightful cycle paths over the next few kilometres, which were, no doubt, built for the very same lovely town dwellers I had just encountered in their cars. Somewhere to relax at weekends… on their bikes.

I had cycled 42km so far and still had 62km to go to the campsite, but just as I was beginning to relax, enjoying the tree-lined cycleway, I was thrown back out onto a busy, winding road with cars, once again, itching to overtake, and me, no doubt, causing quite a bit of irritation for my fellow road users. I wasn't sure I wanted this for the next ten or so kilometres, so I paused at a small intersection and consulted Google Maps again.

Roads are good for getting to places fast, but when the weather isn't great, and drivers are seemingly in a rush, it's not fun and can get very daunting. This was becoming the theme of my day and I didn't enjoy it.

So, when Google showed me another route down a nice-looking lane opposite where I had stopped, I dutifully followed my new directions.

The first few kilometres were lovely, off the busy road with not a car in sight - me and my mate Terence making good headway without any stress. Then, the road turned into a dirt track. Then the dirt track turned into a muddy path across a field, and I was stuck.

Once again, my stubborn man-nature kicked in and said forward, not back, as I muddled through the sticky ground and out onto a forest track. I was still making progress, but it was so much slower than the road.

With no one around and lots of space, I unpacked my drone for the first time on my trip to get some cool video shots. I love using the drone; it creates impressive visuals. The only problem is that I tend to shit myself as soon as I can't see it in the sky with my own two eyes, which with my eyesight, doesn't take very long. To add to the jeopardy, during this bit of filming, I also discovered that it's very good at avoiding things - like trees.

As I set it on one of its automated programmes, it swung off towards the woods but somehow managed to float right through the branches without hitting a single one before coming back out to follow me. All that mild terror for a few seconds of video, which would have been fantastic - me cycling along the track with the footage taken between branches - but, unfortunately, all I ended up filming was me in the background, gawping with panic.

After playing for a while and seeing the expanse of the forest from twenty metres up, it was time to pack things away and carry on down the wide gravel path in roughly the right direction. This was despite Google trying to take me off down sloppy paths every time we passed one, which were still sodden from the morning's rain and barely walkable. As much as I was enjoying cycling away from the road, I now had to accept that I needed to get back on it if I had any chance of reaching my destination today, especially with the changing weather.

So, at the next road junction, I ignored Google's latest instructions to go down a barely walkable path and headed west back towards the road I'd initially come off, straight into a strong headwind.

As I arrived back on the D216 a few kilometres later between Mios and Sanguinet, I checked my computer, only to discover that I had cycled 10km on my little detour and was only about 5km down the road from where I'd left it. My only comfort was that the road had straightened, and the traffic had spread out as I continued towards Sanguinet.

By the time I reached the town, the rain was falling hard, and I was feeling very wet and quite miserable. There was a restaurant at the first junction I came to, so I swerved across, quickly parked Terence outside under a canopy and nervously entered, taking the opportunity to challenge myself once again with my 'stranger in town' routine.

After the customary stares, I bumbled my way into asking for a table and sat my wet bottom on the hard wooden chair. The morning had been long and hard, and by now, I had cycled 72km. Steak and

Chips were just what I needed, along with a fat Coke. So that's what I ordered.

The young waiter started speaking to me in some broken English. I pounced.

'You speak English very well,' I said.

Boom! It worked again, and he started talking more and more in English as his confidence grew.

He told me how he had spent a year in Camden when he was younger. I listened as he seemed to enjoy the chance to speak English. Meanwhile, I was slowly starting to dry out, and thaw out.

Apparently, word has it that French cuisine is one of the best in the world. I always wonder why that is, especially when I am in France, eating French food. The food was expensive and mediocre, and the steak was incredibly fatty, but my spirits had lifted with the meal, and although the rain hadn't completely stopped by the time I left the friendly eatery, it had slowed to a drizzle. I felt full-up and ready to crack on and finish the final 27km to Gastes.

Now, I'm not quite sure what happened next. Perhaps I was delirious from the food, or maybe I was enjoying the lovely little cycle path I'd landed on a little too much. It might have even been the fact that the rain had stopped and the sun had come out for a short while. But, I missed a turn, adding another 8km to my route between Lombard and Goubern. It could have been less, but my mantra of going forward and never backwards was once again my manly downfall. To add insult to injury, the sun said goodbye and the rain returned.

As the afternoon wore on, cycling down dedicated pathways alongside increasingly wetter roads, the rain was very much making its presence felt, and I was ruing my decision - for the first time on the entire trip, I might add - to wear shorts. My feet were squelching in my trainers on every turn of the pedal and my skin was wet from top to bottom underneath my clothes. It didn't feel like southern France.

Somehow, I retained a tiny amount of positivity. Just a smidge. It's always easier to cycle in the rain when you are in the moment rather than hitting it from the off, and sometimes the clouds part just as quickly as they gather. Besides, it wasn't as if I could just stop. I had to keep moving.

I slogged on, getting closer and closer to my destination, chipping away at the distance. It was still only mid-afternoon, but the dark sky made it feel much later, and as the campsite appeared to my left with the lake to my right, I just couldn't bring myself to attempt camping that evening.

I needed hot water and a dry, warm bed. A large Alsation barking without pause outside a caravan near the entrance to the campsite may have also played a part in me consulting the web once again.

As I stopped to do some investigation on my phone, I stumbled across the local Gastes website, which had the strapline, 'A great spot where charm operates everywhere through its authentic and spontaneous inhabitants!' I took a look behind me just in case they were there. They weren't.

But Mimizan Plage, a seaside resort on the Atlantic, looked like the perfect place to head for. It would mean another 20km, but it seemed the most sensible thing to do considering the weather and the lack of authentic and spontaneous inhabitants.

So I booked a room in a hotel, even managing to bag a sea view. (Foolishly, like I did with my ferry cabin, I set my expectations way too high on what to expect.) I also took a gamble on whether they had somewhere for Terence to stay, my new renegade attitude to planning outranking the dull old sensible Craig who likes everything planned and organised.

After 13km more of country roads heading south, it was time to go west and out towards the coast. The afternoon was brightening up again on its rollercoaster journey of weather for the day as Google directed me onto a hilly path route through a forest towards the coast. I'm sure there was probably a lovely flat road to the seaside town, but I did as I was told. Despite the ups and downs, which were becoming a little bit of a struggle after a long day of cycling, it was a beautiful end to my day as I finally smelled the sea air.

Mimizan Place reminded me of so many run-down British seaside resorts, battered by the ocean air. The wind and rain greeted me as I rode into town, and as the hotel came into sight, and with me battered and fatigued from the day, it very much looked like I belonged in this weary old place.

It might not just be the regular battering from the sea, though, that hampers Mimizan Plage's chances of hanging on as a tourist destination. During a quick look on Trip Advisor later that evening, the platform where anyone can gripe about their holiday to get it off their chest, there were two telling clues. Firstly, the top ten things to do in Mimizan Plage, after the plage itself, consisted mainly of day drips elsewhere, although number five was the local tourist office. Secondly, and perhaps more telling, was the consistent complaints about the smell, including Jenn S, who summarised, 'As soon as the wind comes from the direction of the local paper mill, the place stinks unbearably of a mixture of burnt car tyres and rotten eggs.'

The weather today meant that no smell could stay in the air too long before being whipped off to sea at 90 miles an hour. I had got off lightly. It seems the only rotten eggs I would be smelling during my stay would be under my sheets in the early morning.

The hotel was quiet, the small bar empty, but the lady who greeted me was lovely and friendly, quickly checking me in. We locked Terence away in a garage nearby, and I slowly made my way up the thin, steep staircase to my room. All I could think about was how challenging coming down would be.

The room was like an old Butlin's abode, with thin walls, windows that couldn't disguise the outside gales, and a shower cubicle you'd struggle to swing a hamster in, let alone a cat.

Unsurprisingly, the hotel didn't have many guests. But a bed was all I needed, and it was a step up in comfort over a tent, maybe two steps if I was being generous. My sea view may also have been lovely if it wasn't for the wind and torrential rain.

Refreshed and dressed, I headed out to find a supermarket to stock up on snacks. A week had already passed and it would be Sunday tomorrow. I was not taking any chances.

I bought some snacks and water for the day ahead and walked around the town, treating myself to a pizza in one of the few open restaurants. Despite being a Saturday night, only a few sparsely filled bars were open, trying their best to get punters in. It was a bit of a fool's errand, what with the sweeping rain and near-gale-force winds.

Judging by the types of bars and shops available in the centre of the town I passed as I walked back to the hotel, many of which were still shut for the winter, I got the impression that Mimizan Plage was a bit of a surfer's paradise in the summer and that in a couple of months the streets would be full of bleach-blond clones carrying surfboards under their arms, more worried about the wave that got away than the lurid smell that wafts over the town. But, on this wet and windy April Saturday evening, paradise was not exactly the word that came to mind.

127km for the day - 815km travelled.

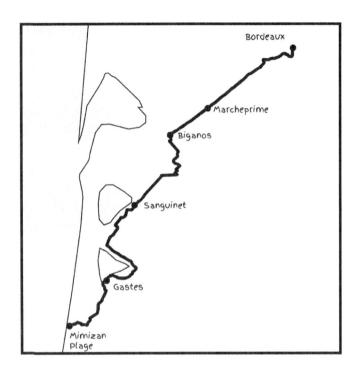

Bordeaux

Marcheprime

Biganos

Sanguinet

Gastes

Mimizan
Plage

Day 10 - Mimizan Plage to Urt

'Have you heard of a guy called Andrew Sykes? He comes to our group.'

With my earplugs well and truly jammed in my lugholes, I slept like a log. It was a cold night, but a radiator in the room offered the dual benefits of keeping me warm and drying my clothes. Surely, it wasn't meant to be like this in late April in Southern France?

I woke refreshed and did my stretches on the bed before making my way down for breakfast, with my buffet expectations relatively low considering the quality of my stay so far. As I walked downstairs, my descent technique was returning to some sort of normality after a whole week of cycling and the steep, narrow staircase was not too much of an issue.

There were some cracking pictures of the resort on the wall from days gone by. Nostalgia is a powerful draw if not a somewhat wasted emotion, but I took my time to take in the town's heydays. I really do wish I could go back in time sometimes, when I see photos like this.

It wasn't the best petit dejeuner I'd had so far on my trip, with only a small selection of pastries on offer, and there was only one other table occupied this early in the morning, by a couple who looked like they'd rather be anywhere else but right here, right now. The quality of the food didn't stop me from taking a Pain Au Chocolat to add to my supermarket stash from the night before. Yes, it was Sunday and I was prepared, with half a baguette ham roll, crisps, banana chips, biscuits, and an emergency can of Ravioli.

Soon, Terence was rolling along the seafront and out of town towards Capbreton, my destination for the day. After yesterday's extra distance, I had a shorter day in store, and it was going to be relatively flat.

The morning air was cool and calm, but the weather overhead looked dark and cloudy, so I still had to don my raincoat over my tee shirt and base layer.

But, as I cycled out of town, southwards over the Courant de Mimizan, the welcoming sky in front of me looked bright blue. Could today possibly offer me some sunshine at last? I could only live in hope. My experience so far had taught me not to get too excited.

As soon as I left the town, past a sprawling campsite, I entered the Landes forest, the most extensive man-made woodland in Western Europe, covering 10,000 square kilometres in the region of Aquitaine. After the horrendous traffic-laden, rainy day before, it was just what I needed - a gentle ride on a wooded path with no cars and very few walkers and cyclists.

The pathway would continue for 61km on and off through a gently rolling landscape that whipped in and out of the forest's canopy. The sun appeared through the trees, and I started to cover a lot of ground very quickly.

I was on the edge of the forest by the coastline, and just to my right was a vast sandbank, which prevented me from seeing the ocean along my journey and the long sandy beaches that welcomed the lapping waves of the Atlantic. It didn't take anything away from my morning, though; it was the most enjoyable cycling I'd done so far on the trip.

Even my journey through the town of Vieux-Boucau-les-Bains was on a dedicated cycle path, occasionally crossing over small roads to continue my journey, passing houses with gardens covered in so much greenery that they camouflaged the built-up areas I passed through, so much so that I nearly missed them.

Making good progress, I was halfway to my destination by late morning. I stopped to chat with a group of older cyclists, and we stumbled around our language differences, me explaining where I had come from and where I was going. It took a while, but we got there in the end before they wished me well and exploded away on their electric bikes, leaving me in the dust.

My beautiful morning of cycling through the forest paths couldn't last forever, though, and after about 65km, I reached the shores of Lac d'Hossegor. My peaceful journey was over and I was back on the roads.

The restaurants were heaving with people making the most of the waterside location for their sunny Sunday lunches, and I found myself weaving around cars, with drivers stopping and starting without a care in the world as they eagerly looked for parking spaces.

Then, on a quieter stretch on the lake's eastern edge, I caught a glimpse of The Pyrenees mountain range in the distance for the first time. Once again, I was having a 'pinch me' moment that made me stop in my tracks. I'd cycled to the Pyrenees from my house in Basingstoke!

I snapped a photo to send back home, which sent my mind racing. It didn't happen often on my trip, but at that exact moment, contemplating my achievement so far, I felt quite alone.

I knew it wouldn't last and that I had to man up, but seeing groups of families and friends chatting away while I knew I wouldn't really speak to anyone for another two weeks hit me. Just keep peddling, Craig.

As I moved closer to Capbreton, things got even busier. It had turned into a sunny afternoon, and plenty of people were cycling and walking on the roads and cycle paths. Children, dogs, and people with headphones in a world of their own started to make life tricky as I ploughed on slowly.

At the lake's southern end, I crossed over the Canal d'Hossegor, the waterway that joins the lake to the sea, and headed west towards the beach to take a look.

I had pretty much reached my destination by now and had plenty of time on my hands. It had only just turned two o'clock as I pushed Terence through the pedestrianised concourse, with its busy bars and restaurants, down towards the large, built-up beach area.

Once again, feeling like a spare part, I found a quiet bench to sit on, eat my lunch and stare out over the sea.

A few people were braving the weather on the beach. It was very sunny now, with a spring-like warmth in the air, and as I people-watched, some folks were down to their swimsuits, running around the beach and braving the water. Others were dressed in thick jackets as if heading for the Arctic.

I was still wearing a base layer underneath my tee shirt and had reverted back to trousers after the wet bath I had taken on yesterday's ride, so I was warm.

With the sun I'd enjoyed throughout the morning, my jacket had come off quite early in the day. I relaxed, unwrapped my solar panel and laid it beside me across the wide wall that divided the sand below from the promenade. I followed its lead and lay down too, taking full advantage of the free power from the sun as I closed my eyes and listened to the hustle and bustle around me for half an hour.

The campsite at Capbreton was less than five kilometres away, and my mind drifted to thinking about the days ahead when I would be crossing over the mountains into Spain. I didn't feel any benefit from stopping now and having a short day, especially when the weather was so lovely. Besides, I felt more than good enough to carry on.

My destination tomorrow was fixed to Saint-Jean-Pied-de-Port, a town on the French side of the Pyrenees that would allow me to break up my climbing over the mountain range to Spain.

So, if I fancied it, I could keep following the coast down towards the lovely seaside town of Biarritz for some nostalgia. I'd visited the area in April 2022 after a recommendation from Ian (yes, him again) after he'd regaled me with story after story over the years about his youthful exploits in the town and how much he loved it there.

Lorraine and I had driven down and stayed in a beautiful house in a neighbourhood that would have passed for the set of an Adams Family movie. The place is gorgeous, with lots of different architectural styles. But it wasn't fully open in April, and there wasn't much to do. You'd think I would have learned from that experience for this trip!

We'd also taken our bikes with us on that trip and had taken a ride north out of the town, through heavy industrial parks and up out to the forest tracks to Labenne before heading inland and coming back around to follow the Ardour River back out to the coast.

If I went to Biarritz, it would mean lots of traffic, lots of people, and another hotel. It would also mean cycling through that horrible industrial area.

So, I decided to head inland. I found somewhere on the internet and pointed Terence away from the coast and towards the hills to chance my arm on a campsite in the small town of Urt.

The sun had been out all day, but I was still wearing my base layer. It wasn't thick, but it added extra warmth as I cycled along in the cool air. But, as the afternoon wore on, I actually started to get hot. So, for the first time on the trip so far, I had to take it off. Yep, finally, here I was on day ten of the ride in my bright pink teeshirt with two pink arms hanging out of the sleeves, wondering what had hit them. Arms, meet sun. Remember him from last year?

Having extended my route at the last minute, I once again had to rely on Google Maps to navigate to my new destination for the rest of the day. Unlike the bike computer, where I could design and load courses with a lot more cycling data, I couldn't see any elevations ahead or what to avoid with Google. So, I just ran with the road, not thinking about elevation, even turning on the radio on my phone at one point to listen to Arsenal beat Tottenham over the radio. It was turning out to be a perfect Sunday.

As I headed inland, the roads became a little more up and down. But, seeing as I was heading towards the mountains, it was mainly up and only to be expected.

Almost immediately, the landscape around me started changing. I was leaving one part of France designed for holidaymakers and heading into the farmlands of hard work and toil. Despite the sun and warmth, it started to feel distinctly Alpine crisscrossing through country lanes and small villages with the Pyrenees as a constant backdrop in the distance, getting ever closer.

As the country roads started to flatten slightly, I arrived at the north bank of the River Ardour on the D74, about 10km inland from Bayonne, the same road I had cycled along in 2022 with Lorraine. Today, though, I'd be heading inland rather than back to the coast, and I burst through the next two flat kilometres rapidly before turning south to cross over the wide alpine-blue river and into Urt.

The town welcomed me with a short, sharp 10% hill, which I managed without wheezing - a step in the right direction of my fitness and a very welcome feeling considering the days ahead.

Five minutes later, I was staring at a campsite sign that said, 'CAMPING CLOSED'.

Caravans and camper vans sat inside the site, and they looked lived in in, but I wasn't sure what to do. My first day of being spontaneous with camping, and it looked like it had just gone shitcakes.

Remembering that there was another campsite close by, I checked online again. There she was - 2.5km across the village. I crossed my fingers, mounted Terence and headed back down the 10% hill.

As I rolled up to the reception hut, I saw people camped up, but the office was shut. I looked at all the signs stuck to the door and noticed one with a telephone number and the word réception. So I called it. A friendly-sounding man answered in French -

there's a first for the trip. He spoke good English after I had proved to him how badly I spoke his mother tongue, and he told me to set up on the small green opposite the wash block. He'd come in the morning to sort out the payment. Phewie of the day!

I pushed Terence over to the small area of grass, ready to sort myself out and set up my nylon home for the night. Another cyclist had already set up camp. He'd taken the best space, complete with its own wooden bench, why wouldn't he? I'd have to make do with an area on the other side of the green.

I said hi, and he replied. He was English, from Halifax. I didn't find out until the next day, but his name was Pete. Ironically, he thought mine was Terence until I coyly told him I'd given my bike a name.

We had language in common and chatted bikes and routes, and I demonstrated my knack for forgetting where I was going and where I'd been – a real pro. Pete had been travelling on his trusty bike, he told me, for over twenty years, although he did describe it as 'Trigger's Broom'. (And if that reference means nothing to you, well shame on you.)

He came across to admire Terence and seemed to know much more about the Genesis Tour De Fer range of touring bikes than I did, asking me questions I couldn't answer before answering them himself. I got the impression he thought I 'had all the gear, but no idea'. To be fair, he had a little bit of a point if he did.

We didn't chat a lot that evening; we just had a couple of ten-minute conversations. It turned out that

Pete belongs to a club of people who all go tour cycling. They get together occasionally, share ideas and have talks. He was stopping off in Urt for the night, having taken the ferry from the UK to Bilbao in Northern Spain, a 38-hour journey he did without a cabin. Now retired, he was cycling across to the south of France and back and seemed to like his own company. I respected that. A man after my own heart.

'Have you heard of a guy called Andrew Sykes?' he asked, 'He comes to our group.'

'Have I!? Yep, he's part of why I'm on this trip in the first place. My girlfriend had one of his books, Crossing Europe on a Bike Called Reggie, which I read and loved. It actually pushed me to organise my own ride.'

Small world.

I love the whole vibe of camping. It forces you to be social, even if it's just nodding to people, which seems to be the minimum requirement. I love the pottering around, moving things from bag to bag, to tent, to bag. Even the can of cold ravioli and half a packet of biscuits for dinner didn't dampen my spirits. I started to think, with the odd sideways glance, that even Pete didn't think I was a complete imbecile.

By 8:30pm, the blue sky had ominously clouded over, and a layer of cool air had descended like a blanket being laid down for the night. So, I retired to my nylon cocoon to hibernate.

I dozed off quite early. But the mixture of a wafer-thin airbed and makeshift pillows gave my arms nowhere to go once again, and I kept waking up with numb arms. For some unknown reason, I took my earplugs out halfway through the night to see if that would help. Unsurprisingly, it didn't. But it turned out Pete's a bit of a snorer, which added to my experience of having an awful night's sleep.

It also turned out that Pete had a really loud alarm that goes off at 6am.

107.5km for the day - 922km travelled.

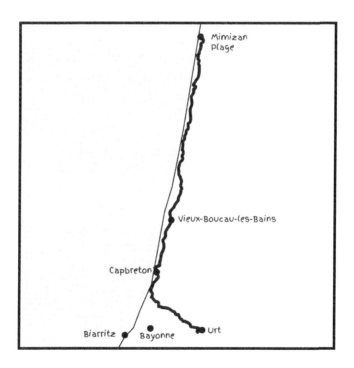

Day 11 - Urt to Saint-Jean-Pied-de-Port

He smiled like a proud child when he told me he'd been planning his adventure for over a year.

At around seven, I finally roly-polyed out of my tent like a stuntman in ultra-slow motion. I lit my gas burner to finally employ my famous dripper (which Lorraine had brought out to me in Bordeaux) for the first homemade coffee of the trip, then I started to pack up my things.

The air was feeling damp, with a few spots of rain, so I rushed to get everything put away as quickly as possible just in case it started to bucket down.

It became a race against time as the spots became heavier and turned to a constant drizzle. I didn't mind getting wet, that was an inevitability, but I didn't want the tent to be damp.

Pete and I said our goodbyes and wished each other well on our respective trips. He looked relieved to regain his solitude. As fantastic company as I know myself to be, I don't blame him; making idle chit-chat with a stranger can be pretty exhausting.

I'm sure I saw him roll his eyes when I caught Pete's attention ten minutes later at the local supermarket. I was stocking up on Coke, biscuits and ready-made rolls; he was weighing fruit.

Then, I was off south towards the mountains and my destination of Saint-Jean-Pied-de-Port. Tonight would be another hotel, partly for comfort's sake and partly because I assumed it would be cold in the mountains, and embracing my newfound spontaneity, I'd decided to book that later.

Having had two days of extending my daily distance, I only had 62km to ride today, and following the early morning alarm call from Pete, it wasn't even nine o'clock as I said goodbye to Urt, my belly full of Pain Au Chocolat.

As if on cue, the skies opened as I trundled out of town. But, despite the rain, I was in excellent spirits, even with 643 metres of climbing ahead of me.

The countryside was green and lush, and the roads were wet and felt like treacle with the running groundwater, so I gave up on trying to keep any part of my anatomy dry.

The first part of my morning meant cutting back across from Urt to the main pass running up into the mountains alongside the River Nive. Through a mixture of hilly countryside roads and small alpine towns, I was in the heart of the foothills of the Pyrenees.

My first stop for un café came quickly after just 12km in the small, picturesque square at La Bastide-

Clairence. Partly to escape the rain for a short while, which was still merrily falling, and partly so I could stare at the buildings, I took the chance for a shot of caffeine in a dry, quiet café.

Set on a steep hill, it wasn't a large square. It had shops and bars on either side, with large arched overhanging brick entrances that created covered walkways on either side, which must come in very handy on days like this. The white-painted facades above had intricate wooden frames and matching coloured window shutters.

It was the sort of alpine town square that an American tourist would go crazy for. It was also the sort of place this British tourist was happy just admiring, making the most of his tiny cup of strong coffee.

My hope that the rain would stop while I paused didn't materialise. I even checked the BBC weather app on my phone, which told me that I should be currently sitting in sunny and cloudy conditions. I gave up waiting after twenty minutes and left, keen to press on.

As I turned the corner out of the square, the postcard view disappeared immediately, like someone sharply pulling a plaster off, with the local factories bursting my bubble. However, the view in that square is one I can still see now if I shut my eyes. It was so pretty.

I was now beginning to hit some short, sharp climbs, including a nice 13% burst that got my heart racing and my legs burning. Anyone who cycles will know how steep that is. Through the town of Hasparren, there was more climbing before descending towards Cambo-les-Bains, leaving me lower than I had started back in Urt.

Crossing the river Nive, it was straight back up again, with a short, sharp climb, leaving me on the main D918 road that would take me all the way to Saint-Jean-Pied-de-Port.

Two more steep climbs into Itxassou and Louhossoa, then the road levelled out to a steady average of 2%; the hard work for the day was done.

My short day was moving fast, and my final 22km up the pass was a gentle climb into the mountains, alongside a railway line and, a little further up, joining the river Nive. It was stunning.

The individual peaks on either side of the weaving pass, each with their own character; the alpine river running by my side - wide, shallow, and rocky as it bubbled along in the opposite direction towards the River Adour back in Bayonne. Despite the morning's rain, cycling wasn't a chore. How could it be? And, although the air remained damp all the way, even the rain had stopped falling.

With the beautiful view distracting me, I made good time, rolling into Saint-Jean-Pied-de-Port at around three o'clock, almost disappointed that my fantastic afternoon of cycling was at an end.

Arriving at the centre of the town, I rounded a sharp bend, cycled over the much-photographed bridge that crosses the Nive de Béhérobie River, and pulled over into a small car park next to the tourist office to assess my plans.

Quite a few hotels I'd been watching throughout the day on booking.com were no longer available, which got me worrying. Had my spontaneity gone too far? 'Mr Big Boots thinks he's The Dice Man now, does he? And now he's got nowhere to stay!'

I bit the bullet and went into the tourist office to ask about hotels in the area. There had to be a few hostelries still that didn't bend to the will of the international traveller with a smartphone app and allowed people to stumble upon them.

The lady behind the counter spoke excellent English. I think I may have mentioned it to her. She gave me a map of the town with a few crosses marking hotels that might have vacancies. This was despite her trying to hide her laugh when I asked about hotels in the first place. It was the sort of laugh that had an undercurrent of 'You've turned up here without a reservation, you absolute arrogant tool.'

I decided there and then that I'd take a room in the first hotel I found.

Through lack of research, what I hadn't realised was that Saint-Jean-Pied-de-Port is the most popular starting point for the Camino de Santiago pilgrimage, an 838 kilometre walk from the Pyrenees to Santiago de Compostela in the Northwest of Spain.

'The Way of St James' leads to a shrine at the Cathedral where the apostle's remains are supposedly buried, and it attracts around 350,000 people each year who want to follow the route on foot. Needless to say, hotel space in the town the walk starts from is quite hard to come by if you don't book in advance, with people arriving daily to leave early the following morning for their adventure.

I cycled around to the first marked hotel on my map, a two-star affair above a bar. I parked up Terence, walked in and asked the woman behind the bar about rooms for the night in my best French. She pointed me in the direction of a desk around the back.

The man sitting behind it spoke good English but seemed a little sheepish when he told me he had only had one room left if I wanted to check it out, as if there may be something wrong with it. It could be a stable and a manger for all I cared right now; I'd take it.

It had a shower, a bed, and a lockup for Terence. I was in, and it's fair to say I was pretty relieved.

The room itself was very basic, which I was used to on this trip, and it had everything I needed. The proprietor even put a heater in the room for me.

I showered, washing my clothes with shower gel at the same time, before ignoring the sign on the heater not to put clothes on it, by laying my clothes across it, as I had a lie-down.

I wasn't quite brave enough to test the device's fire safety, turning it off as I eventually went out for something to eat. After all, I had all night to make the most of the heat source to dry my damp clothes, and as I had thought, the altitude meant the weather was starting to feel chilly. I might actually need it on. That said, I have to question my logic that I wouldn't have the heater on if I was going out, but I would if I was fast asleep, lying next to it!

Saint-Jean-Pied-de-Port was a busy town and very pretty. There were plenty of day tourists wandering around alongside people preparing for their walk the next day. This included a rowdy bunch of young guys at a bar with loud music blaring, which seemed uncharacteristic for the setting and a place I would avoid at all costs. I couldn't help but think they might regret their loud session of beats and booze as they delicately took the first steps on their massive journey across Northern Spain the next morning.

I walked across the bridge with a view, and the next one along on the pretty Rue d'Espagne looking at the Notre-Dame Gate. I looked around the town's back streets before climbing and walking along the wall by the Porte de France next to the main road. It was interesting, for a couple of metres, but not much further. So I came back down to earth as quickly as I had gone up.

As it was still quite early, I walked a couple of kilometres to the large supermarket on the other side of town to get food for the next day. I would be climbing over the Pyrenees and into Spain, and I wanted to be prepared with enough supplies to get me through the entire day.

I was, however, adamant that I wanted to grab a proper meal at a restaurant on the way back to the hotel rather than eat shop-bought food. But, as I wandered back, I soon realised that many of the restaurants were closed. It was only 6pm, but my choices had dwindled. Would I have to eat tomorrow's lunch now and head back to the supermarket first thing?

As I got closer to my small hotel, ready to give in with no restaurants left in play, I noticed a deli. So I went in to buy some sort of delicious, fresh, savoury pastries. I'm not sure what they were, but they sure were nice. It looked like I'd be having dinner in my room after all, washed down with a couple of cans of beer.

Somewhat disappointed as I walked back into the hotel bar, I decided to have a quick glass of beer before I went back up to my room. As I waited to be served, looking through to the back room, I could see people sitting at tables - they were serving food! I could not believe it.

I nearly caved in, but the bar area seemed to be home to an inordinate number of flies. Perhaps a fly convention was in town? So, as much as I'm sure the food was probably lovely, it wasn't the best advert for dining at any level, so I just stuck with a local beer blonde instead.

As I turned away from the bar with my drink, an older guy nursing a small glass of red wine motioned for me to sit with him at his table. I'm sure I'd seen him when I'd left to go out, perhaps even with the same glass of wine. He looked like he wanted some company. Maybe I did, too. So I sat down and joined him.

Through the medium of Google Translate, I discovered he was doing the Camino walk for the next 53 days. I'm guessing he was in his late sixties, and he looked nervous and excited as I read his translated text on the screen of my phone. He smiled like a proud child as he told me he'd been planning his adventure for over a year.

He told me how he'd flown to Biarritz earlier that day and then had to pay more Euros than his flight cost to get to Saint-Jean-Pied-de-Port by taxi. I told him about my cycle ride, but I think he was preoccupied.

We sat there contemplating in silence, a silence only broken by the loud American woman on the table next to us explaining to two compatriots about her messy divorce and a subsequent mid-life crisis that had bought her here to do the Camino walk, now that her children were grown up. Lucky escape for him, I thought as she finally left us to annoy someone in another bar.

We returned to our quiet pondering, two ageing men doing something they'd dreamt of doing for a very long time, perhaps with the realisation that they were right in the middle of their adventure.

No language was required, just a knowing nod. I nursed my beer and then headed up to my room to dry my clothes, eat my pasties and write my diary.

I still often think about that man. Buon viaggio, my friend.

62km for the day - 984km travelled.

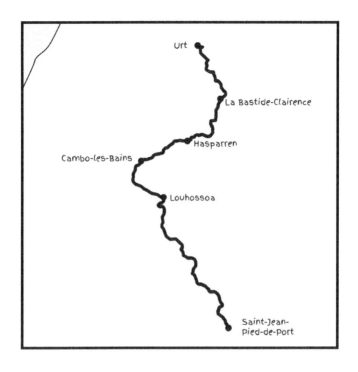

Urt

La Bastide-Clairence

Hasparren

Cambo-les-Bains

Louhossoa

Saint-Jean-
Pied-de-Port

Day 12 - Saint-Jean-Pied-de-Port to Pamplona

I went into the bathroom and made some cream cheese and ham rolls over the sink with my penknife. Bear Grylls, eat your heart out.

My morning started early. The anticipation of crossing the Pyrenees and entering Spain meant it would be a memorable day.

My bedroom, next to the hotel's night entrance, had been eventful throughout the evening. It's incredible how many people walk the halls of a hotel at any time of the day or night with no consideration for the people on the other side of the thin walls. Let's just say, that once again, I was pleased I had brought earplugs with me.

Despite being only 7am, the small breakfast buffet was busy and already being raided by hungry patrons stocking up before heading off for the walk of their lives. The flies from last night were also tucking in, so I quickly made the most of the bad coffee, watered-down juice, hard bread and stale pastries before they shared my meal uninvited. Not even the small selection of meat and cheese looked appetising, which are the things that usually save a boring French breakfast. At least I had my haul from the

Supermarket to fall back on for the rest of the long day ahead.

I was out the door by 8am following my usual bike setup. Thankfully, I now had an organised loading routine: It had only taken eleven days.

Today was all about getting over the Pyrenees. Although I was right on the western side of the mountain range that divides France from Spain, there was still a considerable ascent ahead of me, the bulk of which was in the morning, with around 900 metres of climbing in the first 24 kilometres over the main peak. Two-thirds of those metres were squashed into the final ten kilometres, with an average gradient of around 7%, so the next few hours were going to be challenging.

I was hoping to get to the top of the first main climb by eleven o'clock and I set off from the hotel with the clear understanding that no matter what I thought about the climb - good and bad - it wasn't going to change or suddenly disappear. I just had to grin, bear it, and, most of all, take it all in. These glorious mountain rides are few and far between, no matter how hard they seem at the time.

The cloud was low (or, perhaps, I was just high in the mountains) as I hit a sharp hill on the very first corner out of the town. The low gears would be doing a lot of work today on Terence, and I was simply happy to get distance and metres of climbing behind me slowly. With my bike computer set to what I had left to do rather than what I had done, I would happily watch both sets of numbers - the distance and height - slowly lower as I rode.

Early morning Camino walkers came and went as their route intersected occasionally with the road. My bonjour greetings were returned back with 'Bon Camino'. I wondered if my new Italian friend had started his long journey. I'd think about him a lot throughout the rest of my trip, all the way to Benidorm.

The hills were rolling, but the terrain was more than manageable with my heavy load. The view… The view was stunning. The sun was beginning to rise higher in the sky, with the thinning clouds floating gently in front of the mountains ahead of me, slowly evaporating before my eyes.

It was a Tuesday morning, and my mind thought about what I'd usually be doing back home. My two younger daughters would be getting ready for school, and my colleagues would be settling into their offices. I reminded myself what a lucky boy I was. 'You are on your bike, Craig, cycling in the Pyrenees!'

Eight kilometres into my ride, the road still gradually rising through the mountain valley, I came to the small town of Arneguy, with a steep rockface to my left and houses to the right beneath me. A dog was barking somewhere. I couldn't tell where it was; with no cars around me, the shrill yapping filled the chasm. The road had been pretty empty during the morning as it opened up to the small commercial centre of the town, where I turned right at a roundabout and crossed a bridge, navigating over the river below to continue my journey.

'Ongi Etorri' and 'Bienvenidos' stood out proudly on a large sign by the side of the ride, along with other languages, including British, welcoming me to the Navarra region. I was in Spain. There was no fanfare, no passport control, and… no people.

I spent the next few hundred metres reminding Terence, 'We've cycled to Spain. On a bike, Terence. Spain!' Deep down, I'm sure he was as miffed as me. It was all a little surreal.

The sun had risen by now but was obscured intermittently behind the sharp mountain crops on the other side of the valley, bringing warmth, then pulling it away sharply as it hid.

Three steep kilometres later, I was in Luzaide/ Valcarlos - a small one-street town that looked picture-postcard-pretty. As beautiful as it was, I can only imagine it would be an incredibly dull place to live after you'd got used to the incredible view. I am pretty sure that as soon as children become adults, they desert the place in droves.

The climb into the town had been relentless, so I stopped at a small square just off the road, which acted as a viewing platform over the valley of the pass. As a tourist, I wasn't bored of the view just yet and wanted to revel in it. And boy, what a view it was across the valley.

I parked Terence, walked right to the rail at the front of the platform in wonder, and then looked straight down to see piles of rubbish just dumped on the ground below. Ah.

I stood back a few metres to make the most of my glimpsing visit and tried to forget what I'd just seen.

Across the platform, a hiker had shed his rucksack for a break to take advantage of the same view. Inevitably, we started chatting. He was German, and his English was very good. I told him. Of course, I did. He was on the Camino walk and started telling me this was his favourite place in the world to walk. I could see why.

Back on the bike fifteen minutes later, the climb out of the town was even steeper than the steep entrance I'd just arrived on. We were now in the thick of the mountain climb, and I still had 15km to go before reaching the summit. Usually, that sort of distance would take less than an hour to cycle, but I expected this might take around two.

Luckily, the road up the mountain pass was quiet, although there was the odd lorry to make me wobble a bit. A few cars and camper vans also slowly passed me, engines screaming in low gears, trying to get up the never-ending hill. I trundled along in my lowest gear, with all the screaming taking place in my burning legs.

I was passed by lycra-clad road cyclists. I was passed by people on electric bikes. I didn't care. Another touring cyclist passed me. He stopped for a break, and then I passed him. We'd see each other over the next thirty kilometres and three climbs, taking turns to stop and pass one another like the slowest relay team ever, the one that everyone pity-claps at the Olympics as they cross the line well after everyone else has finished.

The switchbacks in the road started as the hill got steeper towards the top, and I was beginning to struggle. I knew the mountain climb wouldn't last forever as I counted the kilometres slowly down, but I had to start taking regular breaks to catch my breath and give my legs a quick rest.

I wasn't in a rush; I just needed to get there. As I continued up to the summit, my breaks got closer and closer together, like contractions (and just as painful, I'd imagine).

By now, I was concentrating intently on the road markers as my distance guides. It's incredible how much maths you start doing in your head on a bike as you while away the time, trying to take your mind off your aching limbs. 'So, that's the 17km marker, and the top is 8km; so 9km to go. That's 9,000 metres... Or divide by eight and multiply by five; that's, well, five miles and one kilometre. One kilometre is just over half a mile, so let's say five and a half miles. Done it.' Invariably, by the time I'd worked it out... 'Oh, there's the 16km marker!'

It was just a case of keeping my legs turning and the bike moving forward. We'd get there.

Eventually, I turned a corner and could see the top of the climb in the distance. My computer counted down the metres, and, just for fun, it looked much closer than it was. I just kept peddling slowly towards the church right next to the brow of the hill - the Iglesia de San Salvador de Ibañeta - which was, of course, bloody massive, like every church I seem to see. God must be very popular at the top of mountains.

It was around twelve o'clock as I finally steered Terence off the road and into the car park to enjoy the view and stop for lunch. It had taken me four hours to cover the 26 kilometres, including my stops and starts. Having passed the baton a couple of kilometres back, my cycling buddy was already there, sitting at a picnic bench, also trying to get his breath back.

I cycled around the back of the church to the money-shot viewpoint and settled down to rest for half an hour as I ate my lunch and downed a Coke. The vast patchwork blanket of trees hid the road up through the pass - in fact, all you could see were trees - but the view was sweet, more so knowing I had just cycled up here.

People parked their cars, having driven up, all excited to get out and look at the view. I felt like telling them they don't deserve to get out and be excited - that any idiot could drive up here with an engine. I (me and my friend Terence over there) had cycled up here, don't you know? So did my cycling friend over there.

I was being a twat, as per usual.

The air was warm despite the altitude and the sun was shining. I had made it; it felt good. I had cycled up one of the most significant climbs of my trip on a bike weighed down both by my bulk and my kit, including a damp tent and camping kit I'd only used twice on the trip so far. I was beginning to wonder why I'd even brought it with me.

The centre of Spain promised more hard riding like this morning, but now I knew I had it in me, even if it would be at an average speed of just six and a half kilometres per hour.

The route back down the other side of the climb began fast and was enjoyable after the morning's climb, but it was short-lived. Pamplona sits 300 metres higher than Saint-Jean-Pied-de-Port, and despite having cycled upwards all morning, I still had two more climbs to go. I hadn't really factored that into my thinking and just hoped I hadn't peaked too soon, no pun intended.

As I cycled out of the town of Espinal, past a stream of Camino walkers hiking through the streets, peppered with hostels and bars set up for the daily arrivals, I went straight into climb number two.

The Mezkiritz climb was only 66 metres over three kilometres. Still, after the morning's exertions, I really felt it in my legs and was glad to hit the top and start descending once again. Then, it was on to the small town of Erro, after which I had to endure twice the height of climbing over the same distance up to the Erro peak.

I was struggling, as was my relay cycling buddy, each now stopping regularly up the ascent. By now, we were both nodding in appreciation as we passed one another.

The final switchback eventually came, and a sign welcomed me to the top of the day's final climb. My water was running very low, and there was a caravan selling drinks in a lay-by set up for tourists and Camino walkers, the route, once again, joining my own.

A coachload of older Portuguese tourists was parked, and they were out, wandering around enjoying the vista. As I looked for somewhere to park Terence, I assumed my transcendent day of riding had finally rendered me invisible. They each did an outstanding job of getting in my way as I tried to walk across the makeshift gravel car park, and, being old, they also did this very, very slowly, much to my annoyance.

I had yet another Coke, my third of the day, but decided against buying a small bottle of water. The vendor was very much making the most of his van position with his premium pricing policy. I had one full bottle left on my bike and was bound to pass a shop over the next 30km to my Pamplona hotel for a refill.

The final downhill was the nicest of the day and much longer than the previous two. In fact, I benefitted from a slight descent for the rest of the day, although the wind turned a little later, with the resulting headwind removing any advantage the sloping road gave me.

I just kept peddling and made good ground as the road got flatter and flatter, cycling through small industrial towns as the roads widened and the traffic increased. But, I still hadn't passed a noticeable supermarket and was starting to get very low on water.

Coming off the main road at Huarte, now with no water left and starting to feel an urgent need for hydration, I finally hit a suburban area. Thankfully, this led me straight to a row of shops, one of which was a Carrefour Express. At last! I was thirstier than I thought and guzzled down a litre of water as if I'd just come out of the desert after forty days and forty nights.

I was still 8km away from my hotel, but the bulk of the cycling had been done, and I was rehydrated. I enjoyed a casual entrance to the city via a pathway alongside the River Arga, which led me straight to the Ciudadela de Pamplona (the Citadel of Pamplona) and an incredibly steep path that took me up into the old town.

I surveyed the area by the castle wall for a few minutes. I always find these views much more impressive looking up at, rather than looking out from, a thought reinforced as I stared over the drab outskirts of the city with the apex of the Pyrenees barely visible in the distance.

Back on Terence, I twisted and turned through the pedestrianised roads of the old town, past the impressive town hall (the Ayuntamiento de Pamplona). It was a pretty place, if not a little lively, with wandering tourists and local people walking around doing their daily business. What they didn't need was a wide load, riding a wide load, with luggage bags brushing their legs as he bumbled past.

Unfortunately, I'd not chosen a hotel in the old town when I'd booked earlier, so still had another two kilometres to cycle the other side of the old city, out onto the wide Avenue de Pio XII that felt more like the downtown of any large, anonymous American city, complete with standard global franchises on either side.

Hotel Sancho Ramirez sat opposite an expansive park. I had discovered on my trip that with booking.com there were some real bargains to be had and I was taking full advantage, rather than camping. Perhaps I should just throw my tent away? They had a room I could lock Terence in and a room for me, complete with a warm bed and a hot shower. I couldn't complain about the €65 price tag either, as I swiped the key card across the lock and entered my room.

It was a step up from recent hostelries, but someone had obviously smoked in there before me; it did not smell nice at all. I walked straight to the window to pull it open, where I looked down to see they had also used the outside cill as their ashtray. I was immediately confronted by the noise of a school dispersing opposite, with exited children shouting to each other over gossiping parents. It was better than stale smoke, though. Just.

After sorting myself out, I resolved to walk back into the old town to mooch around. I liked the look of the city and started toying with the idea of taking a day off, especially as the weather did not look great for the next day.

So, as I came down through the hotel reception to walk up to the old town, I asked in my broken Spanish about keeping the room for another night. The answer was a swift 'No way, Pedro!'

It was May 1st, tomorrow - National Workers Day - the Spanish equivalent of May Day. The country had a day off, and the hotel was fully booked.

My mind started swirling as I headed out for the two kilometre walk back to the city centre. What was I going to do? Should I look for another hotel, or should I just crack on? I'd think about it for a couple of hours and decide later.

It may have been a cold night for the locals, but it was a warm evening for a boy from Basingstoke. I was the only person wearing shorts and sliders and caught some funny looks as I strolled back up the avenue, past the generically branded restaurants, each sparsely filled with the odd table of youngsters enjoying pizzas, burgers and sushi.

Arriving in the old town, I headed for the Plaza del Castillo. The small, busy streets from earlier were now bustling as families and friends enjoyed the shops, cafés, and bars. It would have been okay if I had been with someone. But, once again, I felt a little lost and overwhelmed. I was not enjoying the busy throng of people chit-chattering away and taking up the full width of the roads without a care in the world.

It's fair to say I don't like crowds at the best of times. Or, as I like to call them… People. I get on my high horse about manners, etiquette, and the lack of people's awareness or mutual respect in public spaces. At home, when I walk with purpose through my local shopping centre, Festival Place, which is something I try to do as little as possible, I forever have to stop dead as rows of women pushing prams chat to each other in a line, phones glued to their hands, oblivious to anyone else who may want to walk on the same path in either direction. As if to make a point, I tend to be quite dramatic as I make my nonsensical silent protest - like a terrible actor in a soap opera - only to get looks and remarks as if I am the one in the wrong.

And don't get me started on mobility scooters blocking entire walkways. Basingstoke must be a training ground for Benidorm in that respect. In fact, there is a greasy spoon café in the town centre, Mr Munch. It must be popular as it's been in there for years, so I can only assume people love eating very basic meals - the sort that take five seconds to cook at home - while sitting in a chair that is screwed to the floor. Perhaps in years gone by, you'd expect a row of motorbikes outside a greasy spoon café. Nowadays, it's a row of mobility scooters. Make of that what you will.

Basingstoke seems to be a mecca for mobility scooters, with hundreds of them at any one time. In fact, legend has it that similar to the ravens leaving the Tower of London, the Mayor will perish if the mobility scooters ever leave Basingstoke.

In the 2010s, I worked in a beauty salon in the older part of the Basingstoke town centre. As was often the case, some of the, how shall I put this gently... Pissheads... Drunks... Alchies... You know who I mean... used to congregate at the benches on the other side of the wide paved area in front of the shop. One of the men was always on a mobility scooter, complete with a dedicated can holder. I can only assume drink-driving laws don't apply, but I don't think that was at the top of his list of priorities.

One day, during a heavy session on a sunny day, he got into a garbled, heated argument with one of his buddies, always a funny thing to observe. As the argument got louder and louder, they suddenly started fighting. He drove around and around in circles, trying to land a punch as his friend, who had a much keener turning circle, just kept catching him from behind. It was both harrowing and hilarious to watch, right up to the point where he crashed dizzily into the front of the salon.

Meanwhile, back in Pamplona, I exited the small lanes and out into the dispersed throng of the plaza. It had the standard feel you'd expect of an historic European city, with a tall, imposing facade that housed bustling restaurants at its feet. As I wandered around the square, I found a bar with a menu printed on the table in multiple languages. It was the ideal place for me to sit, considering the circumstances. Surrounded by couples and groups, I didn't feel lonely, but I felt alone.

When I twisted my neck around to read the menu (I really should have sat on the other side of the table), I opted for the simple Spanish fare of a burger and beer. There wasn't much variety to choose from, but if you go to Tourist Central, you're going to get a menu for tourists. For all I know, it was the Spanish Wetherspoons, if not a lot pricier.

I called my children to catch up with them and tell them where I was. One of them was a bit miffed when I told her I was in Pamplona, where they do the bull running. She got more confused as I explained how they let bulls out onto the streets to chase people who want to be chased. I told her I'd send a video. Later that night, she messaged me back. "Ooooo, I thought you said balls!"

As much as I was enjoying the evening, even on my own, my mind kept thinking about what I would do the next day. I'd started to feel that my plan of cycling through the middle of Spain had to change. I couldn't have a hilly day like today every day for the next ten days, some of which were much longer and much higher. It would be too much. I needed to get back to the hotel and make some plans.

The two kilometre walk back to the hotel helped me clear my head, although I was angry with myself as I passed a few small bars in another part of the old town with the local Pinchos on offer. In hindsight, it was probably for the best. The last thing I needed, with another full day on the bike ahead, was my stomach digesting weird and wonderful cuisine before deciding which end it would come out of.

I passed a small supermarket and went inside to stock up on food. With my newfound understanding of how closed continental countries can be on a Sunday, I was taking no chances with the impending national holiday. By the time I arrived back in my room, I had decided I would leave Pamplona the next morning and head towards Zaragoza and the coast to avoid the central mountains of Spain. Being my original route at the very start of my planning, I knew roughly which way to go; I just needed to plan the specific route.

The next couple of hours involved creating my daily video to post online, which was, by now, becoming a time-consuming chore. Then, it was on to the computer maps of Strava to check out my rerouting. I figured I could get to Zaragoza in two days.

The hotels I could find online dictated that I had to plan a shorter first day to a place called Sádaba before a big second day to Zaragoza. Sádaba had only one hostel and they had a room available. I booked it, and my plan was set.

Then I went into the bathroom and made some cream cheese and ham rolls over the sink with my penknife. Bear Grylls, eat your heart out.

77km for the day - 1,061km travelled.

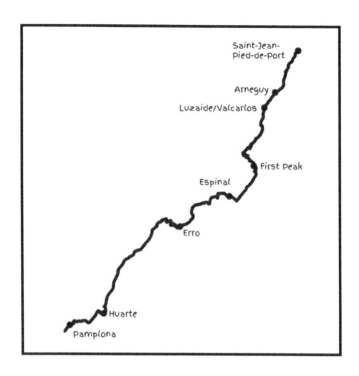

Saint-Jean-
Pied-de-Port

Arneguy

Luzaide/Valcarlos

First Peak

Espinal

Erro

Huarte

Pamplona

Day 13 - Pamplona to Sádaba

I'm not superstitious, and the thought of day thirteen being unlucky didn't even enter my mind. But, by lunchtime, I have to say, it was firmly fixed.

After yesterday evening's stroll into Pamplona, wearing shorts in the twenty degree heat, with the sun shining, I woke up to seven degrees and teaming rain. Such fun!

I also woke up with a dark cloud over me. I'm not entirely sure why, but I felt down. Was I missing home and meaningful human interaction? It had only been four days since I'd said goodbye to Lorraine in Bordeaux, but I felt pissed off and out of sorts.

I honestly don't mind feeling dark sometimes, although thankfully, it happens with much less regularity than it used to in my late teens to mid-thirties. I spent much of the earlier part of that time pondering the age-old questions of 'What's the point of existence?', 'Why are we here?', and other minor queries like that. I probably wasn't much fun to be around during those short episodes of melancholy, but I always tried to hibernate for the few days I felt down against the world.

I even convinced myself (and still have some belief in the thought) that it is biorhythms and the cycles of the moon. After all, if the moon affects oceans, and we humans are basically 60% water, it must affect us. That's my logic. Or my excuse.

The upside of having those periods of darkness was that I read a lot about philosophy and religion and learned a lot about myself. I also discovered The Doors, Radiohead and Leonard Cohen. Every cloud!

Down at the breakfast buffet, I was dragging things out. Watching the rain fall heavily on the patio outside, I just sat in a daze, staring out the window, gorging pastries and baguettes. I could quite easily have packed it all in then and there.

I needed an intervention. So, I returned to my room and got online to chat with the best cheerleader a man could have. Before long, Lorraine had guided me down the cautious path of making me realise how pathetic I was being. It's all part of the adventure, I was told; embrace it!

I can't say it lifted my mood immediately, but it made me realise I was being silly. All I needed to do was get on the bike, move my legs and make sure I was going in the right direction. It wasn't rocket science. My melancholy should disperse during the morning like I hoped the rain clouds overhead would.

I packed Terence up in what I like to call 'Robot Mode', knowing I would soon be walking out into the rain. Robot mode is something I do when I have to do something I don't necessarily want to - like public speaking, making sales calls, or having to watch my children in a school play. You just keep moving forward with or without enthusiasm. Eventually, your mindset shifts or the event in question simply comes and goes. Either way, you get through it.

I took my first tentative steps out of the hotel and into the rain, rolling Terence through the heavy hotel doors as people stood on and watched. 'No, honestly, I don't need help. If you could just stare, that should be sufficient; thank you.'

Being rained on when you're already out cycling is one thing, but actually going out, when minutes before you've been warm and dry, is another thing altogether. I stood under a tree to quickly do some filming for my social media feed, my mood carrying over to the small screen like a method actor. Robert De Niro would have been proud.

As I got on the bike and slowly headed out of the wet city, already starting to feel the rain penetrate my shoes down into my socks, I came across more groups of Camino walkers, this time with ponchos covering their complete bodies and rucksacks. They looked about as jolly as I felt.

I headed south and up my first steep hill of the day into Cizur Menor (not to be confused with the larger neighbouring town of Zizur Mayor). I was cycling so slowly that one of the walkers on the path beside me seemed to be catching me up.

Soon after the town, I parted ways with the Camino walkers for the final time as they trudged west towards North Western Spain, and I rolled eastwards towards the Mediterranean.

Still relatively early in the day, it remained overcast and dark, but the rain had started to slowly lift. So did my mood as I headed for the main climb of the day, which was in two parts. After this ascent, I would have an easier day, all the way to my destination, Sádaba.

The two climbs in front of me weren't long, but with the weight of me, Terence, the cargo (and the enormous chip I was carrying on my shoulder this morning), the first hill felt much more challenging than it should have. Maybe the climbing over the Pyrenees the day before was catching up with me?

I completed the first climb, and my eyes wandered to the village of Arlegui, which sat on my right at the bottom of a large, imposing wooded hill in front. Thankfully, the road I was on ran to the left, going around the edges of the village and the hill rather than through it and over it. And this is where my adventure began.

As I carried on through the village outskirts, large concrete slabs came into view, blocking the road ahead. It did not look good. As I got closer, and now starting to panic, I saw a yellow sign with large black letters: 'CORTADA POR OBRAS'. The one road I had in front of me was closed.

In the cold light of day, on my return home and looking at that part of my trip on a large computer screen, I would learn that there was another road left

I could have ridden to a kilometre or so back. It would have been a detour with some extra distance attached, but it was hard concrete, and that becomes quite relevant as this particular story continues.

But, with the stress of the situation I suddenly found myself in, seemingly in the middle of nowhere with no idea what to do, I made the fatal mistake of trusting Google Maps to deliver me a revised cycling route.

In its wisdom (and yes, I did tell Google I was on a bike), the map plotted a new route that I dutifully followed, bowing to its expertise in the area of mapping, what with it being one of the largest technology companies in the world. It was taking me up towards the enormous hill I saw before me.

I put Terence in my lowest 'granny' gear and trundled up the steep incline into the village. The busy network of minor roads that appeared on the map on my screen didn't seem to correspond at all with what I saw in front of me with my own two eyes, and I found myself stopping to a halt at the first couple of junctions just to calculate which turning to take next.

Ah, that road there, the really steep one that looks like a track. Of course, it's that one! I could see that the local cemetery was further up the same road, so once again, like a lemming, I carried on; it must be a road, surely.

Of course, once I was past the entrance to the graveyard, the track disappeared entirely, turning into two strips of hardened mud. To add to the adventure, the hill got even steeper.

At this point, I had to get off the bike to walk and push Terence up the hill. There was no way I could cycle up the incline.

I wouldn't return to the saddle for a good hour or so.

A hundred or so metres later, the track split into two, and I could see the path Google was suggesting I follow up ahead. It looked like a great path to walk up, perhaps with hiking boots, a rucksack, and some walking poles, but not with 75kg of bike and luggage.

At this point, a more sensible person probably would have turned back. But my in-built stupidity dial ramped up to a Spinal Tap Level 11 and told me, 'No, it would be alright'.

The steep path slowly narrowed through the greenery as the trees and thickets on either side closed in, leaving a rutted pathway with large stones and rocks to navigate. I leaned back, putting my back into it, to push Terence slowly upwards, keeping my legs on either side of the rut for balance.

I felt like I was at the start of a horror movie with me as the main star/victim - a film in which the stranger from out of town walks unknowingly into the misty hill where danger awaits… A danger that all the locals know only too well.

To stop my wandering mind from creating gruesome outcomes, I found a friendly podcast and put it on a loudspeaker to keep me company as I trudged on slowly through the thickening forest.

The stony climb slowly rose 300 metres over the next one and a half kilometres, and the gradient was brutal, reaching 22.5° at some points. With yesterday's exertion over the Pyrenees, I really could have done without this.

The rain had stopped by now, which was one positive, but I was starting to worry about what I'd got myself into and how long it would last. The banality of listening to three ex-footballers talk about football was just about keeping me attached to reality at this point.

Continuing to follow the Google Map directions on my phone, I had no idea when the top of my climb would come. I started thinking about having to descend the hill on the other side, down a similar track, holding Terence back for dear life as he tried to escape my hold down the steep hill.

More than once on the trudge upwards, I got excited that the next slight turn would finally be the summit, as the thick treeline above and in front of me started to thin. Invariably, there was just more pathway, with more rocks, and more up.

Eventually, just as I was giving up hope that the path would ever end, it split in two. The map on my computer screen said to turn left or go straight ahead. There was no straight ahead, just a left and right, so I gambled on going left. I figured I must still be on the left side of the hill so this path, if nothing else, would go around the open side and stop going up. It was a guess, though. I hadn't suddenly turned into Ranulph Fiennes over the past 1,500 metres.

This new path I found myself on was the thinnest of cuttings, but at least it started to flatten out underfoot. As I pushed Terence through the undergrowth, I began to feel sharpness on my left leg. It was thorns nibbling away at my skin. My trusty steed, Terence, was busy protecting my right leg like the bloody trooper he is.

And then I saw it; a stone pathway wide enough for a vehicle just up in front. I nearly cried. To be fair, I'd been sobbing most of the morning, so this was nothing new for today.

I made my way through the last of the brambles and out onto the path, looking down to survey the damage to my legs. They felt damp after walking through the undergrowth. My right leg was fine, just wet. But my left leg was covered in blood, with the added dampness making it look like I'd been in a severe accident.

Using the contents of one of my water bottles to clean it, I did my best to remove the diluted blood, only to reveal a tapestry of red lines, each gently weeping.

At least I had finally come out of the woods, so to speak. I felt like a bit of a hero, especially with the blood running down my leg. I'd been to the precipice and clawed my way back. This was my 'running through the streets of Philidelphia' moment, shadow-boxing and jumping for joy at the top of the 72 steps outside the Museum of Art. But being a hero is all well and good if you have someone to share it with, preferably a crowd or a cinema audience. I just had

Terence, and he sat nonchalantly, not really giving a shit.

As I shook myself from yet another movie scene, I desperately wanted to get back down onto the road and into civilisation. I'd covered nearly two kilometres on foot, and it had taken me an hour to reach the top.

The rough track down the hill looked barely rideable, but on I got, slowly rolling down, looking for the path of least resistance. I just wanted to crack on.

Large clusters of stones and large slippery puddles were the next challenge of the day. It may have been fun on a mountain bike, but poor old Terence was taking a few knocks, and I was struggling for balance. But, the more I descended, the more calm I felt.

Eventually, the trees opened up, as did the track, evening out as I got closer to the foot of the hill, finally arriving at the edge of the village of Subiza.

As I reached the comfort of a real-life street, my ordeal over, I got off Terence and kissed the tarmac. Never again would I moan about a boring old road.

My feet were wet through, my shoes were covered in mud, and the blood on my left leg continued to flow. But, the resolve of getting through this adventure had lightened my mood without me realising. I was back in the game!

I got back on Terence and rejoined the NA-6000, wondering if there were, in fact, any roadworks taking place at all, especially on a bank holiday, and whether I should have just carried Terence over the blocks and carried on.

With a tailwind pushing me along and a gentle downward slope dropping 400m over the next 43km, I started to claw some of my lost time back. For one section, I'm sure I didn't actually pedal for about three kilometres, averaging around 32km/hr for over half an hour.

I cycled swiftly through empty town after empty town, the southward drag veering east along the plains of the Ebro basin.

As I continued, the riding became slightly more laboured with a side wind as the day wore on. Across the flat open roads, I cycled, with the mountains a constant on the horizon, until the small town of Olite appeared in the distance.

As it got closer and closer, there seemed to be the largest of large churches right in the middle, poking its head way out over the rooftops. I was used to oversized churches by now in France and Spain, but I could see it was something special as I entered the town. I turned off the main road to have a nose.

Plenty of people were mooching around in the square as I first set eyes on, not a church, but the Royal Palace of Olite.

Despite being a national holiday, people were out and about, and the bars and restaurants around the tourist attraction were open and busy. Quickly reading up, the Palace was one of the Courts of the Kingdom of Navarre seats from the reign of Charles III until its conquest by Castile in 1512. It looked a lot newer than that. Perhaps it was like Trigger's broom?

Rolling Terence through to a corner of the square, where I could get a good look without getting in the way, I just stood and stared. The Palace was resplendent in its surroundings, and I'm sure some Disney designers could have used it as inspiration as to what a dream castle should look like for their latest princess money-making movie.

I would have loved to have stopped, looked around, and grabbed a coffee or a beer. But, at this stage of the day, and, after the morning's fun, I only cared about getting to my destination and ending the day.

That was Sádaba, and it was still 46 kilometres away. I was just under halfway there.

After heading out of Olite, my ride flattened. Changing directions on criss-crossing roads made me aware of how lucky I had been to have had the tailwind for most of the day as I struggled, head down. Showers of rain would come and go, but by now, my spirit had resurrected. There was no getting me down.

Ten kilometres from the hostel, in the town of Carcastillo, I took one last stop, thinking it might be best to change out of my shorts and cover my legs so I didn't look like an extra out of a Hammer House Of Horror movie when I arrived.

The Hospedería Sádaba was the only small hostelry in a very quiet town. As I rolled slowly through the small streets on my arrival, Google once again took me in a roundabout way, and I began, with an ounce of worry, to wonder if the hostel actually existed. If it didn't, I'd be screwed and probably sleeping in a field.

But, thank heavens, it was where it said it should be, and I rolled up the narrow cobbled street, barely the width of a car, and parked Terence outside the front door after an eventful day of cycling and hiking.

Bugger, the reception was locked.

There was a bar/café next door with the same hostel sign outside, so I walked across and went in. My foreign uncertainty was met, in full-on Spanish, by a helpful young barman. Together, we stumbled through communicating, and he explained that I didn't need to check in; I had a room number and key code in my email confirmation, which corresponded with a room already set up.

Being the sort of person who loves self-checkouts in supermarkets so that I don't have to interact with anyone, I loved this idea. I just had to go to the room number I had been given, and a small key box was outside. Brilliant.

I explained about Terence - not by name, of course, because I can only imagine the confusion that would have resulted - and luckily, they had a sizeable lock-up garage for him, which oddly had circus equipment scattered around the edges.

Sádaba was a lovely little town. The skyline was dominated by a castle and a large church (what else?). I went to explore after my shower to discover, unsurprisingly, that it was a very quiet town and there was very little there.

The castle dates back to the 1100's or the 1300's (they're not quite sure on Wikipedia), but it was no Olite Palace. It was also closed, although this didn't stop a tour guide chatting through its history with a group of onlookers.

From the raised castle, I could see down across the roofs of the town's houses and across to the Iglesia Parroquial Santa Maria. As I wandered back down towards it, through the lanes on the edge of the old town, I passed rows of small houses, some of which were simply facades. Stopping to look through broken windows, I could see the insides gutted with collapsed roofs. It was all rather sad and spoke of times gone by.

The imposing church was tightly packed between houses and small streets. There was no chance of that being left to decay. Perhaps some of the holy budgets of gold and silver and massive churches could have gone towards the local people, who were undoubtedly religious and going through tough times before they were forced to leave their homes.

Old photographs on the hostelry's wall showed days gone by in the town. There were pictures of busy streets and families sitting proudly. There were photos of local parades and events, including one of a group of men making a human tower in the square as large crowds watched on, the man at the top balancing for dear life. Back then, it looked like a fun community to be a part of. But, like many of the towns I had cycled through today, it looked like a town of the past. Deserted by younger generations, heading for larger towns and cities, making it somewhat redundant. Or, perhaps, one by one, the residents had gone for a walk up the road and got lost up a hill in a forest?

Back at the hostel bar, I sat with my new Spanish barman friend, enquiring about food. My body clock still wasn't (and never will be) quite in tune with the Spanish desire to eat late, and I had two hours of video editing ahead of me. So I opted for some tapas there and then, and a beer.

I had returned to my room, I looked at maps to plan my next day. It would be 110km to Zaragoza, where I would take a day off.

I decided to split the difference and opted for a decent day of cycling, followed by a half day to Zaragoza and an afternoon off.

So, my next day's stop would be Pedrola, having found a hotel that fittingly looked like a castle.

89km for the day - 1,151km travelled.

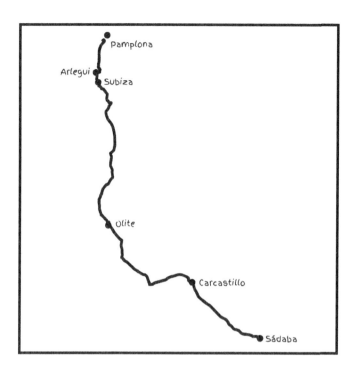

Pamplona

Arlegui

Subiza

Olite

Carcastillo

Sádaba

Day 14 - Sádaba to Pedrola

Knowing my track record of stopping, the Hanging Gardens of Babylon would be just around the next corner.

Despite deciding to split my day's ride in two, I'd still need to cycle 81km today, not a short distance by any stretch.

I woke up having slept incredibly well. But the last few days of riding over the Pyrenees, the stress of my mountain hiking expedition, and the lack of a big hearty meal the night before, had left me feeling a bit jaded as I woke up to prepare for the day ahead.

I didn't need to rush and leave early, so I decided to wait to have breakfast in the café downstairs. As I walked into the quaint little bar that had seemed so empty the night before, with its low ceiling and dark interior, one person was busy trying to serve about eight tables. It felt like an airport waiting lounge. After a quick peek at what the one couple who had been served were eating, I got the impression that the low-cost hostel offered an even lower-quality breakfast - who'd have thought? A carton of orange juice and a croissant in a packet just didn't seem very inspiring.

But I sat at an empty table and waited patiently for ten minutes to be served. In truth, it was possibly only 60 seconds before my lack of patience led me to snatch my room key from the table and head back to my room to chew on the last of my baguette stash.

When I returned downstairs to the café about 45 minutes later with my bags packed and ready to go, the café was empty. I guessed that either the person was quicker at serving than I gave them credit for or everyone else had slightly more, but not much more, patience than me.

I ordered a café solo, and then went off to retrieve Terence from his overnight storage while I left the barman to slowly consider my request.

Six French bikers were already in the lockup, packing up their big, heavy motorcycles. There I was in a tee shirt and shorts, already feeling the morning heat, nodding good mornings to them, weighed down with their layers of thick, protective clothing. At least they didn't have to pedal, I suppose. If they did, they'd evaporate to nothing in their tight, leather cocoons as the day wore on.

I was relieved to see that Terence hadn't decided to run away with the circus. But, as I packed him up for the day's journey, I noticed that one of the panniers that held the bags had come away from the frame. To be honest, it was a bit of a relief. The bike had been rattling the day before, and I thought the bottom bracket issue had raised its ugly head again. It must have just taken a knock on the Ben Nevis-like walk I'd done the day before. (That hill gets bigger every time I tell the story.)

I had some spare nuts and bolts in my toolbag, so I pushed the bike back to the hotel café, parked up outside and tightened it all together over my café solo.

And then I was off.

Warm, dryer weather welcomed me as I mounted Terence and headed out of town. It finally felt like I was cycling in the Iberian Peninsula and not through England in the Spring as I headed for the first hill out of the town. The heat and sun, and potentially a shorter day of cycling, brought on a lovely sense of calm up the short incline. I wasn't in any rush.

With my rations down to a meagre couple of biscuits after my latest baguette breakfast, I decided to add eight kilometres to my day by taking a detour south to visit a supermarket in Ejea de los Caballeros; I'd learned you can never carry too many food supplies on a bike in Spain.

I stopped at the top of the hill, to turn around one last time to look back down at the castle and church, which dominated the small, remote town as they no doubt had for centuries. Sádaba was the type of town I would remember most from my journey, despite not ever feeling the need to revisit in the future.

Then, it was over the brow of the hill, where I was treated with nineteen kilometres of downhill cycling to my first stop, where a short road on the edge of the town took me straight to the supermarket.

It wasn't the biggest shop, but it had everything I needed, and I found myself wandering the aisles of the Mercadona, adding extra things to my basket above and beyond the usual baguettes, water and cakes. I treated myself to some croquettes for lunch and bought a scrubbing brush to clear some of the gunk off Terence's undercarriage. It was easy to overlook that he had had to endure the Kilimanjaro-size climb alongside me the day before.

After paying for my haul, I pushed the bike to a grassy area near the shop, next to the dried-out river bed of the Arba de Luesia, a shopping bag hanging off each side of the handlebars.

It wasn't as lovely as it sounds. The grass was very dry - thirstier than me, I'd say - and a dumper truck was busy dumping not too far away on a noisy building site across the road.

The morning was heating up as I downed water, filled bottles, scoffed cakes and scrubbed Terence's nether region. It was nice to have time on my side. It might have been even nicer if I was next to a flowing river in a village or by the side of the ocean, but hey-ho.

I often find myself stopping on trips, either by bike or car, just a little too hastily at a stop that sits just before the really nice one. I'll take a break by the edge of an industrial estate or at the smallest service station on the planet - the kind with one picnic bench right by the side of the road - only to find the Garden of Eden a few kilometres further on. It's got to the point where taking longer car trips in the UK sees me doing a little research upfront or asking for recommendations. Who says I'm getting old? If you're ever heading north on the M6, by the way, you really must try the sausage roll at Tebay Services.

Fed, watered and cleaned, back in Ejea de los Caballeros, I found myself getting caught up in a one-way system as I headed back out of town. I thought I knew roughly which direction I was going (like a man) and failed (also, like a man), before finally ending up back where I started. Then, after a quick reversion to Google Maps, which for once didn't want to guide me up a mountain, I was finally heading out of town through a small industrial area before landing on some quiet country roads surrounded by farmlands and acres of Almond trees.

Travelling southwards, I had occasion to head east and then north for short stretches on the twisting lanes, only to be faced with terrific headwinds, which made me realise how much of a help the wind was being behind me. Looking at the map, I saw a more direct route using a main road, but I was really enjoying my day away from cars while, luckily, remaining firmly on concrete.

This being Day fourteen of my ride, my body was now used to the daily exertions. The cycling was enjoyable and much less demanding, even with Terence's weight and the bags. I was finally on the journey I had pictured for months before I left Basingstoke, and I had a spring in my step.

It's human nature, I suppose, to time travel in our minds to future events we have planned. I find that I do it a lot. Invariably, it's wasted; things never happen the way you think they will. In fact, I often find myself looking for problems in future situations rather than thinking about the joy they may bring.

The question, 'Craig, do you fancy going to see that band you love in London?' leads my mind to think about parking or travel or how busy it will be and whether I'll manage to get to the bar or not. Or, if I'll get stuck standing behind Peter Crouch, Greg Davies and Stephen Merchant on a night out. This all happens in a matter of seconds before I invariably decline.

This cycling trip was weakening that thought process daily. I was turning up at hostels that I'd booked the same day with no idea what would happen with the bike, or, knowing if the place even existed.

A significant learning I'd had - if I had to encapsulate it in a best-selling self-help book - was that, in general, people simply want to help if they can.

We're so used to seeing awful humans on the news or hearing about horrible social media attacks that we assume people are generally horrid. People, I was finding, by and large, are decent. (As I wrote that, I remembered the guy in the Jag in Hampshire and want to add a caveat: At least 50% of people are decent.)

I stopped at around 40km to have lunch just outside a small village called El Sabinar, next to the Río Riguel. Once again, it sounds lovelier than it was. I parked Terence and stood by the side of the small, dusty lane, eating my croquettes, once having to move out of the way as a lorry trundled past, covering me in a cloud of dust. Knowing my track record of stopping, the Hanging Gardens of Babylon would be just around the next corner.

Fifty metres after lunch, there was no luscious garden, but I was back on a main road and flying down to Tauste. As I approached the town 20km later, I saw the route in front of me veer to the right and around the outskirts of the town, which sat proudly on a small hill in front of me. But, I was fascinated by the tower of the Parroquia de Santa María, yet another imposing church dominating the skyline of a town, so I turned off and cycled up towards it.

I'm not entirely sure it was the best use of my time as I navigated through the tiny one-way streets, only to find the 13th-century church and stare at it for approximately sixty seconds before leaving.

Cycling back out of the town, once again being led this way and that, through narrow one-way streets, many of which were cobbled for extra fun, I found myself being spat out only a little further down the road from where I'd left it. At least I was back on track, and I knew which way to go.

This turned out to be right around to the south side of Tauste in a wide circumference. If I'd dropped out the back of the town from the top, I'd have saved myself a few kilometres.

The rest of the day's ride was down a fast, busier route, through half-empty towns until I crossed over the railway running alongside me twenty kilometres later. This took me into the Pedrola and through to

Hotel Castillo Bonavía. My ride through the village and down a quiet (very missable) lane was uneventful until I was confronted by what looked like a medieval castle in the distance, the Hotel Castillo Bonavía Pedrola.

It was like a cross between a Disney hotel and Crossroads motel, and despite me approaching it from a quiet country lane, it backed onto the very busy A68 Autovia del Ebro.

There was no Miss Diane or Benny to greet me, and the reception was incredibly slow at checking me in. I didn't even have Meg Mortimer to complain to. But at least the walls felt quite sturdy.

After finally being given my key card, about fifteen minutes later, I was told that Terence would stay in the room with me on the balcony.

So I removed the pannier bags and took them up before coming back down for Terence. The staff seemed to think he'd go in the tiny lift to take him up to the first floor, so I had to balance the bike on the front wheel (the back wheel had a mudguard preventing me from raising the front wheel too far) and squeeze it into the lift, with me squashed to the side, holding on to the back wheel for dear life, lifting it as high as it would go. I'm sure I didn't look strange at all, despite a group of people watching on in amused wonder.

The hotel room was nice and big. It also had a bath! I'm not afraid to say I bloody love a bath, so this hotel was already shaping up to be my best one yet.

It also had a wide patio door that led out onto a lovely balcony where Terence would be staying. The green matting and garden furniture were encased by a wall built to resemble a battlement. The castle vibe was somewhat lost when I looked out over my kingdom, though, when I was rewarded with a view of a Cepsa petrol station by the side of the motorway, right in front of me.

I had a quick shower so that I could go downstairs to take full advantage of the sunny weather and the bar, where I did my late afternoon video editing session aided by an ice-cold beer. €4.50 for a glass, though (£3.85)! It felt expensive at the time but seems quite cheap when I say it out loud, now.

I'd still not got used to the pricing out here, either in France or Spain, with cheap beers and only €1.40 for a coffee in a café. The problem I had was that people speak so fast in bars and cafés when they ask for payment that I always give them notes because I have no idea of the number they just asked for. Then, when they give me loads of change, it catches me by surprise, and I give them a huge tip, probably costing me more than if I were a pub or coffee chain in the UK.

Hotel Castillo Bonavía was trying to be something it was not. While they had young, expectant couples in, overawed at the decor, having cosy chats with the Wedding Planner in the corner of the bar, there were also groups of nattering workmen, pairs of engineers with branded polo shirts, and travelling couples on a stopover. It doesn't matter how many swords you fix to the wall or suits of armour you display; if you are by a motorway, even if your hotel looks like a castle, you won't attract knights journeying on their latest quest; just sales reps.

The dinner in the hotel was good, the best meal I'd had on the trip so far, barring French Ian's rustic treat, and I retired to my room around nine-thirty, tired and ready for bed.

But, I had been placed next to a family room which seemed to house two parents that didn't give a shit that their children were batshit crazy and bouncing off the walls. Not for the first time, my earplugs came to the rescue.

81.5km for the day - 1,231.5km travelled.

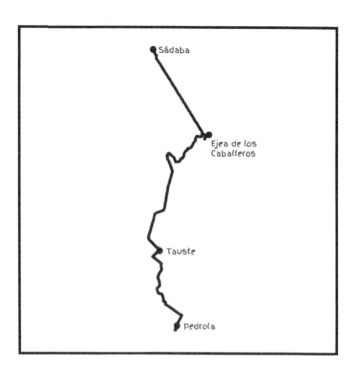

Sádaba

Ejea de los
Caballeros

Tauste

Pedrola

194

Day 15- Pedrola to Zaragoza

'What size beer you ask? Large, of course. I'm British.'

I was quietly enjoying my breakfast with the other early-rising workmen and travelling sales reps when a family bounded through the door. Judging by the way the boy looked like he'd just entered Willy Wonka's Chocolate Factory, pointing at the bounties at the breakfast buffet, I assumed it must be my neighbours from the room next door.

The parents, both dragging their feet and carrying large bags under their eyes, sat the children down, quickly making them chocolate milk and laying out some cakes from the buffet on the table. Yeah, that'll calm them down.

At least it kept them quiet and still for a short while. I ignored them, finished my baguette, pastry and coffee, then moseyed back to my bedroom to get ready. Ironically, as I passed the family room next to mine, a 'Do Not Disturb' sign was hanging on the door handle.

I had a short day of cycling today with only 39km down to Zaragoza, which I imagined would take me less than three hours. So, I decided to take advantage of the bath for my first dip of the trip, and I slowly prepared for my day.

I was going to camp tonight for only the third time on my journey. Zaragoza had a municipal campsite, the weather looked warm, and I was feeling brave.

I packed my bags and took them to reception, returning for Terence, who was easily carried down the wide staircase in a much less degrading manner than his journey up in the lift the afternoon before. Then, I slowly peddled away from the Castillo hotel on the same quiet lane I'd entered, back to Pedrola at a very late 10:15am.

As I left the hotel grounds, I noticed a helicopter in a field to my left. I hadn't seen that on the way in, and I certainly had not heard one land, so either it was a stealth helicopter, or I had been my usual observant self on the day before. I was flummoxed for a good thirty seconds trying to work it out as I carried on down the lane, confused and wobbling slowly.

Less than two kilometres into my ride, having journeyed back to the outskirts of the village, I was guided off the road and onto a canal pathway.

It was stony but flat, and I soon got into my stride, neither fast nor in a rush. I was on the Canal Imperial de Aragón, a 110km waterway fed from the nearby River Ebro and built in the late 1700s to irrigate local farmland, just in case you were wondering.

Stale sections of the canal didn't hold the best smell that morning, but what it didn't possess in beautiful aroma, it made up for in the shape of walls of midges.

Hundreds (if not trillions) of these little flying irritants left me spitting every few metres, and I was glad to be wearing glasses. They seemed especially attracted to the sun cream on my arms and legs and the Vaseline on my lips. I was, quite literally, a cycling fly trap as my arms started turning black with sleeves of midges.

After twelve kilometres, the canal entered the Acueducto del Río Jalón, a two kilometre stretch of aqueduct next to an intersection with the river Jalón running below.

I found myself on a path guided away from the raised waterway towards a small cluster of picnic benches and a country lane leading away from the canal, and it was nice, once again, to get back onto the smooth tarmac as I cycled away.

In fact, I was so excited, trying to figure out the route ahead in the distance, that I wasn't really paying attention to the map on my bike computer. One kilometre later, I realised that I was going the wrong way altogether and had to retrace my route back to the picnic benches.

I found the turn I was meant to take between some trees, one that you could blink and miss (as I had just proven), and I got back on track towards Zaragoza, running once again alongside the canal.

But, I immediately hit a little snag - The Jalón, the river underneath the canal. There was a crossing in front of me, but it wasn't a lovely bridge; no, that would be too simple. I came face-to-face with a ford, a good foot or two deep and stony underfoot.

I could go back to the road and cycle right around; it would be a fair few extra kilometres. Or, I could remove my shoes and socks, hope my balance was up to scratch, and push Terence across.

It's worth pointing out at this point that despite my Maradona-esque physique (post-playing career), where apparently a lower centre of gravity is a good thing for balance, I do tend to fall over rather a lot.

As a youngster, it never used to bother me. As a kid, I loved falling over. It was a hobby. But, since getting older - and I can not pinpoint the exact age; I'm sure it didn't just happen overnight - it seems that falling over is now a near-fatal experience. Just another worry to add to the Sniper's Alley that is my fifties.

To add insult to injury, I now also tend to fall over in slow motion. It's as if I know what's coming but decide to have a little falling-over foreplay first, as a tease, just to get myself in the mood, giving me plenty of time to worry about what part of my hefty body is going to take the most impact.

What hurts most about this is that I used to actively make time to watch old people fall over on the video clip show - You've Been Framed. It was my favourite section of the show. The shock, the drama, and the (lack of) speed as a sixty-year-old woman took five to ten seconds to fall over at the family barbecue. It had me crying with laughter. Will she crush the patio furniture? Fall over the children's toys? Nope, she's face-planted the fence panel and gone right through to next door's garden.

But now, that's me. I have become that person. In fact, I could probably earn £2,500 a week from sending in ten clips a week from my life. But, alas, after 32 glorious years, the show got cancelled in 2022. I guess the Internet took over, and I can't be arsed to go searching for 'old women falling over' videos just for a giggle (I just tried; it's not quite the same).

I don't think it could have been the production costs that ended the show. Despite running for 23 years, they never paid more than £250 per clip. That's despite inflation based on the show starting in 1990, which according to the Bank Of England, meant I could have been earning £5,446.70 a week for my ten videos today.

Back at the river, off came my shoes and socks, and I secured them high up on the bike so they didn't get anywhere near the water. Tentatively, I edged Terence towards the water, trying to work out the shallowest, least rocky pathway, and prepared to take my chances.

Five minutes later, with not a slow motion slip in sight, my trainers still fully dry, and I was sitting on a jagged rock face on the other side of the ford, wiping small stones and grit from my feet and putting my shoes and socks back on. I felt like a true adventurer as I banked another short war story to regale people when I got home. In fact, I'm sure that river will be as deep and wide as the Nile by the end of the year.

Turning left, then right, then left again, I was once again riding alongside the aqueduct. The gravel path returned with no water under foot or wheel; just more stones, dust, and plenty of flies.

And that's how it continued for most of the journey, as I passed the airport on my right, with squadrons of fighter jets taking off and making me wobble as I turned to watch them.

Luckily, the canal path was quite wide; otherwise, I may well have been sitting in stagnant water with flies circling my head.

As my 40km journey neared its end, I entered the outskirts of Zaragoza from the southwest, still on the same meandering canal path, riding under massive concrete flyovers covered with graffiti and through thin, low tunnels under local roads. Then, it was time to cross the waterway over a small footbridge and cycle away from the track. I was less than 2km from Camping Ciudad De Zaragoza.

My tiny tent looked strange between the camper vans, set on the edge of a substantial pitch on the campsite, but by 2pm I was set up and showered with my washing already drying in the afternoon sun. I could either sit here all afternoon, or I could cycle seven kilometres into the city centre to have a look around.

The cycle path network into the city centre was fantastic. Even though the wide roads were busy, there was a dedicated space for bikes and the many cyclists and scooter riders going about their business. It felt good not working to a timetable or heading for a destination, and it was just what I needed. Terence felt as light as a feather without the bags as we navigated our way through the busy city streets and into the centre of the city.

We took in the closed Aljafería Palace before I sat in awe over a drink in the square opposite the Basilica of Our Lady of the Pillar, as Terence stood under the trees nearby. It really is a beautiful building.

This is my preferred way of doing sightseeing on a city break. I don't need a guide or a bus tour; I just find a bar, preferably with a beer (but today with a Coke) and just sit staring. Then it's a case of 'TICK, done that one!'.

After half an hour of sitting, sipping and gawping, we left, dawdling through the streets, dodging people with cameras wandering along in a world of their own, soaking up the Catedral del Salvador, the Arco del Deán, the Monumento al Rey Alfonso I el Batallador, and the Estadio La Romareda, the footballing home of Real Zaragoza. I've travelled around cities twice this year on a bike; it's such a relaxed way to get around and see stuff.

Once again, feeling a little out of place, I decided against having a meal in the city's tourist area, opting for a trip to the Supermercado on my way back to the campsite. It was Friday, and I would be heading into unknown regions of Spain the next day; well, unknown to me. Having already experienced

Sundays and bank holidays in Spain and France, I was taking no chances and stocked up on bread, cakes and biscuits, along with a balanced athletic dinner of croquettes, salad, crisps and beer.

When I returned to my tent, my French neighbour in the camper van beside me had returned from his day out with his wife. We chatted for a while. It looked like he was the social one in the relationship; she stayed well away.

I drank my two beers, ate my croquettes, and then decided to go to the campsite bar to have another beer and catch up on some admin, taking full advantage of a table and chair, something I was missing in my small camping plot. I also took advantage of some free electric. It was still sunny, and thankfully, the bar was quiet.

'Beer!' I asked of the young guy serving. He looked about twelve. 'Size? Large, of course. I'm British'.

The beer that arrived was enormous, about the size of a baguette folded in three - baguettes now being my new form of measuring reference.

'How big is my tent, you ask? Oh, about two baguettes by five and roughly a baguette and a half high.'

The beer was so large, in fact, that I needed two hands for the first few sips. It didn't help that it was in the flimsiest of flimsy plastic cups, approximately two crumbs of a baguette thick. But I was settled for an hour or two and ready to crack on with my work.

Other people started arriving for drinks, and the tables began to fill with small families and groups of friends chatting away. I say chatting; it was more like shouting.

Spanish people sure know how to talk loudly to each other. At one point, I felt like walking over to one family and pointing out they were less than two baguettes away from each other and to turn it down a notch or two. Instead, I just put my headphones on and thanked my lucky stars for my quiet French neighbours back at the pitch. After the family in the hotel room next to me the night before, I'd hate to be on a camping pitch next to these families in the bar with no walls to dampen even the slightest sound.

39km for the day - 1,271km travelled.

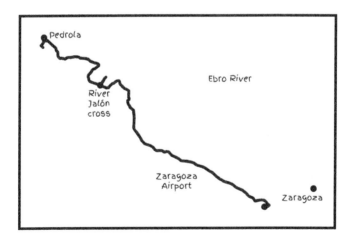

Day 16 - Zaragoza to Sástago

I wondered if I should send a message home before I crossed, telling everyone I loved them; just in case.

My third night of camping on the trip had been the most successful. It had been warm, and I'd enjoyed the best sleep in a tent since I'd been away. That said, it was also the third worst sleep I'd had on the trip - you do the maths. I decided I just don't have the right build for sleeping in a tent. Or, indeed, a decent air bed or pillow.

I reconciled the fact that if I ever made a trip like this again, I'd just resign myself to the relative luxury of a hotel room - not that any had been that luxurious so far - the result being that I'd sleep much better each night and I'd have a much lighter bike.

I woke around 6:30am, well before all my neighbours in their nice warm tourers and caravans. As I roly-polyed out of the tent, still not managing to look anything other than foolish, I felt a couple of specks of rain starting to hit my skin, so I hurriedly dismantled and bagged up my nylon home so it would remain dry.

I made myself a coffee, ate a substantial roll and continued packing away the rest of my kit, by which time my French neighbour was up. Steaming coffee in hand, he sauntered over for a chat in his dressing gown. The social conventions of camping mean that there is nothing strange whatsoever about strangers sharing small talk in their night clothes.

I think men change when they are camping in this respect, transforming seamlessly into a manlier version of themselves who, paradoxically, are much more comfortable in more revealing, perhaps less manly, situations - such as having a chat with a complete stranger in pyjamas.

I have a vivid memory of my dad in one such situation on one of our family camping trips back in the eighties. We were in the south of France at a favourite site at Cavalaire-sur-Mer. It had been raining hard for a couple of days, and we were stuck, as children, running between the tent and the clubhouse, trying not to get bored without the nearby beach to play on.

During a break in the rain, I was pootling back to our tent, wet drops still slowly falling from the branches of the overhanging trees, when I saw my dad walking straight towards me, off performing some sort of chore.

Now, bearing in mind that he was quite a conservative kind of fella, I found it quite odd, walking down a leafy lane alongside people in raincoats and with umbrellas, only to see this man I looked up to with full admiration, wearing just a pair of small, skimpy swimming trunks and some sandals.

When I asked him why he wasn't fully dressed and was only wearing trunks, his reply, which encapsulates most men of that era, was, 'I didn't want to get my clothes wet'.

Back at the campsite, my French neighbour asked me about my route from the UK and where I'd crossed the Pyrenees. I told him about my day from the French side in Saint-Jean-Pied-de-Port through to Pamplona.

'Non, non, non!' he replied, impressed, telling me he'd driven up that road before, so he knew it well.

The respect was reciprocated silently. My new friend had a wonderful moustache; with the shape, size and density I could only dream of growing myself. I'm not talking about any kind of moustache, by the way. I have a particular 'type'. For instance, I don't carry dreams of decorating my upper lip like Burt Reynolds, Salvador Dali, or Adolf Hitler, for that matter. No, my new French friend carried his moustache like Wilford Brimley.

Now, if you were born in the seventies or before, or have a penchant for eighties movies (or lovely bushy moustaches), you'd know Wilf from the movie Cocoon, a film about a bunch of old people in a Florida nursing home who discover alien pods in the swimming pool of the empty house next door. One day, they break in, swim in the pool and feel like youngsters again. Needless to say, if you hadn't guessed already, it's a bit science fiction'y.

Despite being surrounded by more prominent ageing actors like Don Ameche, Jessica Tandy and Brian Dennehy, plus a much younger Steve

Guttenberg in his prime, Wilf stole the show for me. He was pragmatic and commanding within his septuagenarian cohort, and, as a spotty 14-year-old desperately waiting for fluff to form on my chin, I was sure the route of his power and wisdom was all down to that moustache. I wanted one and was prepared to bide my time.

My problem is, even at the age of 53, I still can't grow one like that. Whenever I've tried, I just end up looking like a double-glazing salesman from the 1980s. I also find facial hair very annoying if it grows too long. It takes on a life of its own, storing bits of toast and crumbs and ending up like a fluffy lucky dip requiring constant scratching, even when it's not itchy.

The irony is, and I have only just found this out (and it's blown my mind somewhat), Wilfred Brimley was only just turning 50 during the filming of Cocoon, so I have three years on him. It looks like my moustache dreams are over for good!

Here I was, chatting away to a French stranger, avoiding eye contact by gawping at the space between his mouth and nose, with my pathetic two weeks of beard growth, probably the equivalent of his five o'clock shadow. But, I had to eventually pull away my magnetic stare, it was time to say our au revoirs.

Out of the campsite, I cycled back down to the canal path, rejoining it at the exact same point I'd left it the day before, to continue my journey onwards.

The stony path snaked through the heart of the busy city for five kilometres, before edging me off onto roads where I started to climb out and away from Zaragoza.

In general, I found that, like Rennes earlier on my trip, city folk just don't have the same friendliness to strangers. Most of my hola's were not reciprocated by the many joggers, lycra-clad mountain bikers, and a large number of people begrudgingly taking their dogs for a morning walk, staring at their phones in a daze.

A large, busy road up and out of the city offered a quiet cycle path that ran alongside it, and before long, I was on the outskirts of the city, finding myself directed onto another path beside a new canal as I continued my journey in a southeasterly direction.

The track was rough as I tried to find the smoothest line. This was made harder with a number of groups of elderly women with walking poles, taking up the entire width of the path while they chattered away, begrudgingly moving at the last minute following my liberal use of the bell.

As the morning wore on and the heat of the day rose, my human obstacles became sparser, and I was soon well away from the outskirts of the city and in the middle of nowhere, and heading into deepest, darkest Spain.

After 24km of canal path, I reached El Burgo de Ebro and was back on the tarmac, saying hello, once again, to the River Ebro, which had run the same route as me from well before Zaragoza. I was following the river basin, so it was only to be expected.

My now wobbling arms thanked The Lord as I smoothly sailed along for a few kilometres on flat, quiet roads.

At 910km, the River Ebro is the longest river in Spain. Emanating in Fontibre, south of Santander, the river meanders across the country in a slight southeasterly direction, finally entering the Mediterranean Sea midway between Barcelona and Valencia, just east of Amposta. I wasn't to know it yet, but I would make a strong acquaintance with the River Ebro over the next few days, and we'd cross paths many times on my way towards the Spanish coast.

The lovely, quiet road didn't last too long, feeding me out onto a larger road, which, in turn, led me to an even larger one. I soon found myself cycling on the N-232, part of the Carreteras nacionales network, similar to A-roads in the UK. I had already encountered N-roads on the Spanish leg of my trip, but like A-roads in the UK, they offer very different experiences. Some are lovely single-lane roads, not too busy, and some are busy dual carriageways. And, very much like the UK, some have incredibly complex roadworks taking place.

That is where I found myself, nudged up against a tight barrier preventing me from staying out of the way of the cars on the relative safety of a hard shoulder. The 1.5-metre distance rule was ignored as car after lorry after car whizzed closely by my elbow. I felt like I was back in England. Nothing was slowing down, especially my heart and bum hole, which were now racing away like Lewis Hamilton!

Eventually, after a few nervous kilometres, a slip road beckoned. It was my escape off this horrible road and a welcome respite, so I veered off towards the town of Fuentes de Ebro.

It wasn't the end of the pressure, though. The ramp off the main road rose to the right before bending left in a large arc and across a bridge back over the main road, and the roadworks continued up the first part of the rise, leaving only a narrow passage for cars, lorries, and in this case, bikes.

As I trundled up the shallow slope, I could feel the pressure immediately as a long line of cars and trucks started to form behind me, screeching away in their low gears like a cacophony of revved-up mopeds being ridden by sixteen-year-olds. At the first tiniest available lay-by, somewhere halfway up the ramp, I pulled over to let them all pass and to allow my heart rate to slow a little.

There was a Supermercado immediately on my left as I entered the town, so I took the chance to quickly stop for a cold can of Coke and some sort of pasty and to recover from my little ordeal. It wasn't Lidl, but it was very much trying to be, judging by the washing powder and patio set the couple had in their trolley in front of me.

Cycling out the other side of the town in a southeasterly direction, the route on my computer was guiding me straight back up onto the N-232 at a connection that looked suspiciously like a motorway junction. Following my very recent journey on the same road, hanging on for dear life, I didn't really fancy it, so foolishly (when will I learn), I consulted Google for an alternative route.

It looked 'roady' on the map. It looked 'roady' in front of me. I also didn't have many options. It was either this or the N-232. So, I bit the bullet and followed Google's advice, desperately needing some cycling with fewer cars and lorries to contend with.

Five minutes later, the 'roady' road had turned into a a bit of a 'bumpy, stony' track. Once again, like the stubborn idiot I am, I didn't turn around.

As I continued, the track became smaller, turning into a path running alongside the main train line between Barcelona and Madrid. Although I assumed it must be a key railway connection between two major cities, it was a simple, raised single line with no protective fences. As I bounced along slowly, only one train rattled past, and I kept telling myself that tarmac would return again soon.

But then I reached a point where the path in front of me just stopped at the edge of a field, with only crops ahead, right up to the ballast of the line with no way through.

Looking across the line, I could see a path on the other side of the train track. I would either have to cycle a few kilometres back or just lift my bike and cross over the railway line. By now, dear reader, I'm sure you've guessed which option I chose.

I had visions of a shoe getting stuck on a track or part of the bike getting caught up on the line with a speeding train towards us. I wondered if I should send a message home first, telling everyone I loved them, just in case. In the end, it took less than ten seconds to clean lift Terence across the track. After all, it was only about five baguettes wide.

Tarmac arrived a few kilometres later, and I turned right, wondering where my route would lead. Would it be another rubbly track that disappeared halfway along? Or, perhaps, a lovely smooth country lane? The answer came after just 200 metres when I rejoined the N-232 four and a half kilometres down from where I'd left it and hour before. I was getting fed up following Google on mad goose chases like this. Yes, it added to the overall adventure and gave me stories to tell, but it really was wasting large chunks of my day.

By now, the road had become single-lane and much quieter with traffic. I was also relieved to see a lovely, wide, hard shoulder. Perhaps now, I could get back on track and make back some lost time.

After half an hour, the road led me into a town called Quinto, where I decided to stop for lunch. I'd seen an image of a lovely little square online with a bar to one side. As luck would have it, there were actually two bars in the square, side-by-side. As Craig's luck would have it, they were both full of locals with not a spare table in sight.

Quinto was a small town, the sort of place that probably doesn't see tourists very often - a town where strangers are approached by locals saying, 'You're not from 'round 'ere, are you?' - a bit like Overton or Whitchurch, small Hampshire towns just outside the metropolis of Basingstoke, where I live. So I decided to retreat.

I looked around the small tree-lined square, The Plaza España, which was encapsulated on three sides by the Iglesia de la Asunción (a huge church, of course) at the back, the town hall to the right, and the two bustling bars on the left. I quickly found a shady bench under some trees and sat down to eat a baguette and cool off for a while. It was sweltering in the midday sun. Despite that, I chuckled to see some of the locals walking around wearing puffa jackets, no less.

A man came and sat on the bench opposite me. He had opted for a less-stylish anarak, rather than a puffa jacket. I should have guessed what would come next as he started mumbling away, excitedly repeating himself over and over again.

Back in the day, I guess he would be classed as the village idiot, but obviously, we don't say that now for fear of being cancelled. Anyway, the village idiot started rambling and pointing to Terence. I tried to knock him bandy with my Spanish… 'Lo siento, soy Ingles. No entiendo' ('Sorry, I'm English, I don't understand.'). So, he started talking louder and faster. This must be what it's like for a foreign waiter when an English tourist tries to order a meal in a resort restaurant, I thought.

I understood that he was asking about my bike, but that was all I could understand from his ramblings. I was starting to worry about how I'd get out of this situation with any sense of comfort or without being arrested. He just kept talking at me as people walked by with their heads down, hats and scarves wrapped tightly around their person in the sweltering heat.

Luckily, his wife/sister/carer bounded out of the town hall, calling him over like he was a ditzy pet blindly chewing mud, and he was gone as quickly as he had appeared.

And so was I, stocking up with water and sweets at a small supermarket as I left the town to continue my journey, making the fatal mistake of forgetting that tomorrow was Sunday and that I was entering the backlands of Spain. It would come back to haunt me.

Out of Quinto and I soon had to turn off the now empty N-232, to follow the path of the River Ebro towards my destination for the day, Sástago.

The afternoon was getting very hot. Maybe it was even warm enough for the townfolk of Quinto to get down to two or three layers? I just crossed my fingers that the hostel I was aiming for was real because I felt very isolated heading into the wilderness.

The landscape was beautiful, as was riding by the wide river. But, with rivers come commerce, and there were some big plants along the way by the banks - not the green ones, the ones that make concrete and stuff like that.

I stopped to make a video of myself cycling over a bridge, attaching my camera to the road barrier. It's always fun to stop and cycle back and forth a couple of times, looking into the distance, pretending the camera isn't there, just to get five seconds of extra footage.

With my nonchalant cyclist movie role complete, I stopped on a track by the side of the road to retrieve my camera. Two older guys on electric touring bikes stopped alongside me and started speaking away in Spanish very fast.

When I explained (badly) that I didn't speak Spanish, one of them started to tell me not to trust Google Maps. I think he thought I was just about to follow the dirt track I had stopped on, and they'd obviously made the same mistake as me at some point. I said gracias, and they shot off in the same direction I was heading.

When I arrived, Sástago was surrounded on three sides by the River Ebro, meandering its way through the baron landscape around the town. It was only small, with one long road through the middle of the town, which was so tight it had traffic lights at each end for one lane of flowing vehicles at a time. The lights took an age to change and I sat waiting for a good ten minutes. Or maybe, more likely, it was one.

Considering the town was so small, it took me longer than it should have to find my hostel, cycling backwards and forwards a few times in the afternoon heat looking for road signs to tell me where I was. I was starting to worry that it didn't actually exist.

But, after a couple of drive-bys, I finally found the right road, let out a little sigh of relief, then quickly found the hostel, my home for the night. It had a bar attached, so the first port-of-call was to grab an icy beer and call home.

Sástago was very quiet, and it looked like the bar was the centre of all action. After my routine of showering and laundry, I came back down for another icy beer to be joined by three other people.

But it was Saturday night, and by eight o'clock, at least ten people were appreciating the delights of the bar and outside patio.

A multi-generational family seemed to be enjoying an evening out, including two young children waddling around in every direction, bumping into tables high on sweets and pop. One of them, who I'd guess was around four years old, was busy chewing on the edge of a packet of cigarettes his nan had given him to play with. It felt like I was in a social club in seventies England.

The good news, though, was that the bar also had a small restaurant. The double good news was that I managed to get in without a booking. When I walked in there were just two other people - a French couple.

A two-course meal, plus a large bottle of water, only set me back €12.50. I even had the pleasure of a giant TV in the corner of the room, on full blast, showing an American hospital drama, complete with close-ups of gory scenes in an operating theatre.

Yummy, yummy. The perfect accompaniment to dinner.

Thank heavens for the two courses, though, even at €12.50. I've never been served so few chips for a meal in my life. I would have asked for a discount, but I was too full up from the bean and chorizo stew starter that was enough to feed four people with some leftovers.

After dinner, I retired to my bed early, dodging the pair of pinball toddlers as I walked back through the bar, and slept like a log, ready for my last serious day of prolonged climbing in the trip.

77km for the day - 1,348km travelled.

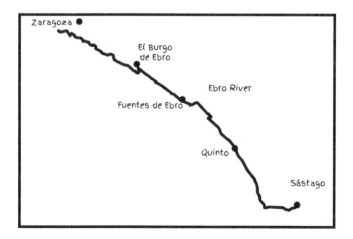

Day 17 - Sástago to Valjunquera

For some reason that I still can't quite fathom, I made the somewhat foolish decision to ride up to Calatrava Castle.

Having been told the previous night that the bar would be shut for breakfast in the morning, I was somewhat surprised to come down the stairs to be greeted by the manager busying himself behind the bar.

I had just eaten one of my stash of rolls for breakfast in my room, and it would've been good to have saved that and eaten breakfast here. But a coffee would have to do. Not only was it Sunday, but it was also an isolated region, just to add to the jeopardy. With hindsight, I should have paid him to make me a roll or two, but it just didn't dawn on me at the time.

As I fixed my pannier bags to the frame of the bike in the small reception area, two pairs of legs in shorts came into view on the stairs. As they gingerly descended, walking in slippery cycling shoes, their bright yellow tops slowly appeared from the waist up. It was my two cycling buddies from the day before.

Walking over, they said hola and stood admiring Terence close up, chatting in Spanish as they pointed at bits on the bike. Who could blame them? He is a bit of a stunner.

José, the one who could speak English a little better than I could speak Spanish, asked me about my destination for the day. I told him I was heading for Batea, about 73km east. Despite being on electric bikes, they were travelling much shorter distances than me each day. Their destination for the day was Caspe, only 30km away. I'd like to think I went up in their estimation as they chatted to each other in Spanish on my response; it was hard to tell with the language barrier. Either that or they just thought I was mad.

They wandered off into the bar and ordered some breakfast as if to highlight my lack of knowledge as a travelling cyclist in Spanish hostelries. 'Look, Craig, a yummy breakfast to prepare us for the day ahead, what with it being Sunday and all!'

With my bike all ready to rumble, I followed them in to finish my coffee and order another.

José and his amigo were chatting away in Spanish, pointing at his phone, probably planning their day. I stood wondering if I'd enjoy that experience right now, having to share the responsibility of planning a day with another person. Most of the time, I like planning routes on my own, and I was very much enjoying my solo riding experience. I'm not quite sure that after two weeks alone, I could be that compromising.

With my café solo downed and my caffeine stores upped, I went back out to leave. As I tightened straps and stretched bungies over bags, clipping them to panniers, José walked over to me excitedly, phone in hand.

'You must go here,' he said, pointing at his screen. I tried to understand what he was saying as he spoke in Spanish, but he spoke too fast for me to comprehend, and the website he had on his phone was also in Spanish, so I couldn't read it.

I looked at the web address of the page he was trying to show me and typed it into my phone to translate. It was a disused railway track –

The Camino Natural Vía Verde de la Val de Zafán. That one conversation, and possibly the longest ever name for a path, would be the making of my entire trip.

There are several Via Verdes in Spain - old, disused rail routes that have been transformed into paths for cycling and walking. Initially built for trains, the routes were obviously designed with smoother gradients, complete with tunnels through the rocks, as they headed inland from the coast and up to the mountains, crossing picturesque and often barren landscapes to connect remote towns.

José showed me his route on a map. They were looking to pick up the trail in a couple of days.

Through single words and hand gestures, he continued explaining why it was worth me heading for the track and that I wouldn't regret it.

There was no way I was going to ignore the advice, so I hastily retrieved my computer from its pouch, sat down with yet another coffee, and completely replanned my day.

I found and booked a hostel close to the start of the marked Via Verde route in the town of Valjunquera. The distance and climbing were similar, so my day wouldn't be too different, and although I'd lose money on the hotel booking I'd made the night before for today, I was all in.

José was pleased with his intervention and started telling me more about his cycling adventures in general and how he'd once cycled in America. I didn't really catch the drift and soon got a little bored, as his English was only marginally better than my Spanish. He even gave me a business card (it was more of a business slip of paper than a business card, really) with his personal details on it, including the web address of his Blog. I read it later and it was equally as boring.

With my day's new route loaded onto my bike computer and my hostel booked, I set off out of the village and over the southern stretch of the Ebro, straight onto a hill parallel to the river. Ten minutes and a lovely switchback later, and the time still only about 8:30am, I was drenched in sweat as I paused at the top of the climb to look back down across the meandering River Ebro to Sástago.

Was this a new me? Mr Spontaneous. Changing plans at the last minute felt strange, but it also felt right.

The morning's cycling was pleasant. I knew I had some climbing today, but the metres disappeared over the undulating landscape, as did the kilometres.

I crossed the Ebro downriver once again, heading south into Escatrón, my route much more direct than the river, and I continued towards Samper de Calanda.

The road was quiet and smooth, and I made quick progress. The scenery was stunning, and I stopped to take some photographs, which did no justice whatsoever with the view I could see with my own eyes. So, I just deleted them.

As I arrived at the outskirts of Samper de Calanda, complete, of course, with a humungous church dominating the skyline, my map told me to turn left. I couldn't see much of a road there but obeyed, only to be immediately confronted with another stony track.

The track would continue for 16km, and it was only later, when I did some research, that I realised (and it made perfect sense when I did) that this was also part of the same Vía Verde de la Val de Zafán, higher in the hills and much further inland than the old train station I was aiming for that marked the start of my journey down towards the coast.

The surface was nothing like the one I would get used to the following day. This portion was designed for walkers, not touring bikes called Terence carrying a load of baggage and a pink sweaty English man. It was liberally covered in gravel and stones across the full width of the path, making the cycling slow and cumbersome. I looked for worn tracks to make the peddling easier, but every time I moved across, I seemed to see a better one somewhere else across the path, like an illusion, and none of them really made any difference.

It's funny looking back - with the information I found out sitting at home in front of my computer a few weeks later - because so much more about that route makes sense now: The small bridges over ravines and gullies, the cut-throughs in protruding rock formations, the shallow gradients, and the derelict hut-like buildings, which would have been small stations.

I remember it being incredibly hard-going and seemingly never-ending, leaving me feeling quite isolated at times. With nothing much to think about except peddling forward, my mind had started to wander, especially at the ridiculousness of the scenario - a 53-year-old man, not known for his adventurous spirit, cycling in the middle of nowhere.

I was pleased and relieved when I eventually hit the tarmac again at a small village called Puig Moreno, passing old people sitting on benches under the large tree canopies in the late morning sun, their faces bemused as I said buenos dias.

My average speed for the day had come down somewhat after the 16km track ride, and the pressure felt like it was ramping up for the day. I'd received a message from the hostel where I was staying that night telling me they would be leaving at 4pm and that I'd need to call them if I was late. I now had a deadline I wanted to hit. Besides, they had a restaurant, so I wanted to make it there in time to get some food.

The lunchtime heat wasn't helping my hydration and energy levels, but a quick stop to eat the last of my rolls and down a Coke pepped me up. I was also down to the last two bottles of my water supply and only had some random cakes and biscuits to get me through the rest of the day.

14km of smooth roads later, and having been spat out again on my old friend, the N-232, I hit the town of Alcañiz, which was bustling with tourists.

The bars were busy and full of people enjoying a Sunday afternoon drink and tapas in the central Plaza de España, in front of the imposing Iglesia de Santa Maria La Mayor De Alcañiz (a bloody big church, just in case you hadn't guessed).

I was tempted to stop but was wary of the time and wary that I was a tourist on a bike that didn't fit in. I only had 22km to go and could eat at the hostel when I arrived.

For some reason that I still can't quite fathom, I made the somewhat foolish decision to ride up to the Castillo de Alcañiz o de los Calatravos (Calatrava Castle). This was, unsurprisingly, perched on a steep central outcrop that dominated the town - ideal for a perfect castle lookout back in the day, but not so much for a ladened cyclist. 70 metres of climbing over 1km later, some at which was 19% (by which time I had to get off and push), I was surveying the surrounding area, trying to understand which way I would be heading. It looked hilly in all directions, but I knew that from looking at my bike computer. As for the castle, it looked like it had been converted to a hotel.

Keen to get on, I shot back down the hill, hanging on for dear life. My brakes screamed for all they were worth trying to hold back the weight of me, Terence and the luggage. Then, back on flatter roads, I headed out of town, almost tempted by one last restaurant. No, Craig, it's not far now.

As I said goodbye to the outskirts of Alcañiz, heading towards an imposing hill and a busy road in front of me, there was a huge sigh of relief as my computer directed me off to the right and onto a road which headed straight for a tunnel through the hill.

But, of course, as was fast become the way on this trip, that road soon turned to a track, and once again, I was on rough gravel, complete with a constant 2-3% climb for what seemed like an age.

The heat was scorching, and my food and water supplies were depleting fast. (This track also turned out to be another section of the Vía Verde de la Val de Zafán I would find out later).

I trundled on slowly, now listening to Podcasts to distract me. The town of Valdealgorfa appeared high up in the distance as I carried on climbing slowly. Eventually, after what felt like hours, I hit the tarmac again, just north of the town, and straight onto four more kilometres up an even steeper hill.

I knew it was the last climb of the day, but my legs were shot, and my energy was low. It was slow going, and I had to stop a few times to get my breath back and rest my tired legs. Valdealgorfa, which had seemed so high an hour ago, was way down behind me now as I finally arrived at the top of the hill, joining an intersection of, you've guessed it, the N-232.

There was a café. It was open, and I was tempted to stop. I wish I had. But it was now 3:50pm, and I still had 4km to ride to the hostel. It was a fast downhill, so although it would be tight, I felt I could still make it by 4pm.

Off a slip road on the other side of the N-232, it was lovely drifting down towards my destination, Valjunquera, having done so much climbing during the day. It was so attractive coasting, in fact, that I cycled straight past the hostel for a few hundred metres and had to turn back when I realised I'd completely missed it.

I'd made it. I was tired and hungry.

I entered the bar, and a group was just finishing their dinner. The food looked good, as did the menu.

I explained who I was, and then we had fun and games trying to check in because the card machine wouldn't connect online to accept my payment. This continued for about ten minutes as the couple serving tried to take payment with my phone and two credit cards. The guy talked about a storm the day before being the problem; his wife took over and sullenly blamed my cards.

Just on the verge of them saying, 'Sorry we can't help you, you're screwed and in the middle of nowhere', I checked my wallet and realised I had enough cash to pay. I would rather not have to use it, but I had enough money left for tomorrow when I would need to find a shop that was open to restock.

'A que hora por comida', I tried. Nothing.

'What time do you finish food?'

'Ah, kitchen finished. They go, we close.'

I eyed up the stale cakes and ice cream cabinet. With hindsight (once again), I should have ransacked the place, but I asked if there was food in the village. 'Oh yes, in the village,' came the reply.

Two hours later, washed and rested, I discovered he had lied or simply not understood. Valjunquera was a beautiful village with small, tight lanes and nooks and crannies that no car would ever be able to corner. But there was no bar or restaurant to be found. I just hoped that the tiny shop I passed in the centre was really a shop I could use in the morning, although it looked suspiciously like a house.

Having taken a little walk around, I decided to return to my silent bedroom in the deserted hostel, where I sat and ate the last of the biscuits and pain au chocolats from my bag and washed them down with water from the bathroom sink.

73km for the day - 1,419km travelled.

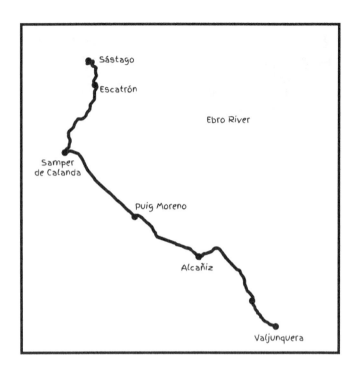

Sástago

Escatrón

Ebro River

Samper
de Calanda

Puig Moreno

Alcañiz

Valjunquera

Day 18 - Valjunquera to Amposta

I tried to style it out for a minute before the rain got heavier, leaving me gingerly walking over the greasy floor in my slippery flip-flops.

As mentioned earlier in this book, in May 2017, I cycled up the Col du Tourmalet, an iconic pass in the Pyrenees mountain range often used in the more challenging stages of the Tour De France. I still have such vivid memories of that ride. I remember the eager start at Luz-Saint Sauveur and the laughs of some local guys enquiring what a group of (all but one) overweight, middle-aged fellas were up to, all dressed in lycra. To be fair, only one of us looked like he might make it to the top without medical assistance. Three of us were also sitting, drinking a beer with our breakfast; the laughs were fully justified.

The four of us split up immediately as we left the village and hit the beginning of the climb, and we were each left to our own little personal journeys up to the top - both physically and mentally.

It took me two and a half hours to force myself up the 1,455-metre climb, which is relenting over the 20.5-kilometre distance. Even now, I have such graphic pictures of various parts of the ride in my head. The intense hill coming out of the village of

Barèges, the expansive car park area by the ski lifts, the switch-backs towards the top of the climb, and the final turn, with a punishing gradient pushing 15%.

I also remember a vulture circling me at the top of the climb for a few kilometres as if he might just stick around to see if I made it or not.

It was spectacular - a lifelong memorable experience - and I will keep replaying it in my head for years to come. It was also surprisingly emotional. If you've ever been on a ride like that, you'll know exactly what I mean.

Seven years later, on this sunny day in North East Spain, I would not shift the Tourmalet from the number one spot - after all, it is the Bryan Adams 'Everything I Do' of my top ten cycle rides - but it would enter straight into the top five. It was glorious.

The café in the hostel was thankfully open when I came down early, and I enjoyed a chunky cured meat baguette and coffee. It was good to get some proper food at last and, luckily, I still had some cash on me!

It was Monday morning, so the shops would be open today, and I wouldn't have the same dilemma as the previous day finding food, as long as I could find a town along the sparsely populated route. In fact, yesterday would be my last Sunday of the trip, so it would be plain sailing from here on in all the way to Benidorm - I hoped. I pinpointed the town of Cretas, about 27 kilometres into my day, where I could restock on snacks. So rather than wait for the local shop to open and hope it wasn't just someone's front room, I said adios and decided to crack on.

The first part of my journey away from the hostel led me up through the outskirts of Valjunquera for three and a half kilometres to what would have been the old train station. I'm not entirely sure why, but this would be a theme of the Vía Verde de la Val de Zafán: Train stations, now abandoned, each a few kilometres away from the towns they served. Perhaps that's why the train line died out? People got bored of walking to the station.

The old, deserted station houses sat high above the path, the old track. Seeing these historic buildings with so many stories to tell left to ruin, overgrown with plants and graffiti, was sad but poignant; thinking about what used to be. Those meandering thoughts and the arid Spanish landscape surrounding me added to the romantic notion of being in a Wild West movie location. That said, my primary Western movie reference is Back To The Future III. It's not really the same. Perhaps I was just reminiscing about all those Sunday mornings watching Little House On The Prairie. Or, perhaps, I need to start wondering why I try to liken so many of my life's situations to movies or TV shows.

The path was smooth and balanced as I rode off, with soft turns and a gentle decline. After yesterday's climbing, I would be descending around 600 metres today, winding down towards the east coast. Still high in the remote hills, the path was quiet, and I took full advantage of light peddling over eleven kilometres of gentle downhill before the track inverted to a 2% climb for the next eleven kilometres. It was easy cycling, though. The mixture of tunnels, viaducts and pathways cut out of the mountains meant that every hill - up or down - was gentle. It was no Tourmalet, but I couldn't take my eyes off the panorama surrounding me.

With my incline complete, the next fifty kilometres was downhill, apart from my short supermarket stop at Cretas. When I arrived at the old station stop, two kilometres from the town, I left the track and headed onto the road leading up to the town, which stood proud at the top of a steep hill in front of me that looked harder to climb than it ended up being. Perhaps having cycled every day but one over the past two weeks had helped my fitness to unexpected, new levels that I wasn't used to.

Once again, I relied on Google Maps to guide me to the supermarket off the main road through the town. The streets quickly narrowed into a maze-like centre, similar to Valjunquera the night before.

Following tight twists and turns, I pulled up outside the shop after a few minutes, parked Terence and parted the fly curtain to walk inside and see what was available. Despite being called a supermarket, there was nothing super about this market whatsoever. It was tiny. But it had the basics, and that's all I needed to feel comfortable again with my supply levels.

These last few days in Spain had left me feeling isolated, away from the large towns and cities. I felt like an alien - the travelling cyclist from England - an oddity. Everyone was friendly enough, but I felt very much out of place. But, to be fair, I feel that way quite a lot in England, too.

Thinking about these situations, where I had found myself lacking food, drink and open shops over the past few days as I crossed Spain straight towards the coast, I realised that I had made the right choice to change route back in Pamplona. I imagine riding down the centre of Spain for the next few days would have meant more of the same.

I was having mixed emotions all around this morning. Perhaps I was starting to feel a little lonely? As much as I was enjoying the entire experience of the ride itself and not being someone who craves company, the end was approaching fast and was starting to play more and more on my mind. I'd spent sixteen of the last eighteen days on my own, sleeping in a different place each night, and it was turning into a routine despite glorious days of cycling like today. But, I'm sure if I had Facetimed Lorraine right now, she'd tell me to man up and enjoy every peddle stroke for what it was. And she'd be right. So I did.

After packing my brand new stash of biscuits, crisps and, for some reason, some frankfurter sausages, I downed an ice-cold Coke and filled my water bottles, keeping an extra two-litre bottle in my pannier bags for the afternoon. Five litres of water added a lot of weight to the bike, and I felt the balance change as I mounted Terence to make my way out of the cute

Spanish town, taking full advantage of coasting down the big hill I'd just climbed up on my way back down to the station.

Back on the Viá Verde, I carried on through more stunning scenery. Outcrops of huge mountains in the distance, highlighted by the late morning sun, continued my sense of riding my trusty steed in a Western.

Some of the disused train tunnels were lit, and some weren't and were quite rough under the wheels. It was exhilarating for all the wrong reasons every time I went from bright sunshine into darkness, not quite knowing what to expect as my eyes tried to adjust quickly to the sharp change. It meant slowing right down each time I entered a tunnel just to work out where the side walls were. After all, I didn't fancy scraping myself along a rocky wall, especially in the dark.

Terence's lights were coming in handy, but even they struggled to lead the way through the darkness of some of the longer tunnels, and extra jeopardy was added if you happened to have cyclists coming the other way in the dark. Some had no lights at all; some seemed to be carrying the front beams of a lorry. It made for an energetic experience.

As I entered the more mountainous part of the route, which winds its way around to the north of the main range of mountains that seperate the coast from the inland plains, the tunnels came thick and fast. Overall, my speed was slower (I was still trying to avoid hitting tunnel walls), but I was having a fantastic ride with so much to look at.

During one section of the track, I cycled out of a tunnel to be confronted by isolated rocky alcoves on all sides, with stunningly clear, deep waterways in the rock formations below. It's fair to say that you simply would not be afforded views like this sitting in a car travelling, and they demanded that I stop and stare for a few moments to take it in. I felt privileged to be here, as isolated as it was, seeing natural beauty that very few people get to see, albeit on a manmade construction.

Abandoned stations came and went as I descended further down the route. The tunnels became less frequent, the rocky mountain pass faded slowly behind me, and the landscape became gentler.

After 65 kilometres, the Camino Natural Vía Verde de la Val de Zafán had started to level out. I found myself converging next to the River Ebro, which had slowed and widened as it neared its rendezvous with the Mediterranean. Perhaps the exact same bit of water I saw yesterday was now flowing next to me on its journey towards the sea?

I still had to decide where to stop for the night, but my first option was Tortosa. I was at sea level, and the terrain had finally become flat. I was finally leaving Spain's interior and heading for the bustling coastline.

Eventually, turning off the Viá Verde just outside Tortosa to the North West, I felt a little sad, like an exciting journey was over. I'd like to go back and do it again another day and share the experience with someone. Or visit one of the many other similar routes around Europe.

I stopped by the side of the road and retrieved my phone to check hotels and plan the rest of my day. It was still only two-thirty, so I decided I would continue to the next town, Amposta, to make tomorrow slightly shorter. It was only another seventeen kilometres, so I'd still be there with plenty of time to relax.

I opened booking.com to book a hotel, but having found a suitable location to select, the App decided it didn't like my payment cards - a bit like last night's hostelry - as I went to confirm the booking, which meant I'd need to stop and use my computer instead. So, I headed into the centre of Tortosa to find a café and take a break.

A busy town, with the Ebra running straight through the middle, the town promised much in my imagination, having checked out the photos on Google Images earlier in the day. It didn't live up to the hype whatsoever, and it was hard to pair the lovely pictures online with what I now saw in the cold light of day.

I was also struggling to find a restaurant or suitable café to stop at in the centre of town. There were just shops, mostly of which were closed. Having given up, deciding to leave the town and carry straight on through, I finally came across a restaurant on the road out of town. In fact, I stumbled across a whole row of them. It was time to stop and relax.

Having not had a proper cooked meal for a day or two, I ordered a steak and a Coke and fired up my laptop. I did a search, found the same hotel, chose a room and booked it with no card issues whatsoever. Easy.

A few minutes later, with my laptop still open, I got the confirmation email. There was a bit of a problem. Despite booking.com refusing my payment card on the phone, it had kept the original room booking in the basket from my earlier attempt, and I'd just managed to book two identical rooms in the same hotel!

Websites like booking.com made it incredibly easy for me to organise accommodation as I went along. But how would it fare now that I had an issue? The quick answer was 'not well at all'.

I spent twenty minutes on the phone trying to confirm my details and explain myself to someone, only to be told that they couldn't even find my booking in their system. Having stopped to relax, I felt more tense than ever as I cut off the call.

I would just have to cycle on and sort the issue out when I arrived at the hotel. I may also have to swallow the extra payment.

The bill arrived for my meal. It was €15 for a steak, chips, and a drink! At least a little bit of luck was going my way.

The cycle ride from Tortosa to Amposta was flat and fast. First, down a busy dual carriageway out of the town before heading off at a roundabout onto a narrow side road. This, in turn, forked off onto a dedicated cycle path, and I eventually found myself cycling back on a gravel track sandwiched between a canal on one side and the River Ebro on the other.

I arrived in Amposta at around 4pm, crossing over the river on a very tight bridge and into the centre of town. The hotel was small, and the staff were fantastic.

After mentioning to the lady at reception how good her English was, I explained the situation regarding the double booking. She smiled, cancelled the booking and sold me one room at the same price. Considering the issues I'd had, I was so grateful and vowed to lose booking.com more commission as I continued my journey by booking directly with hotels.

Terence joined several bikes already parked up in the meeting room for his overnight stay. Perhaps there was a cycling convention in the morning? I retired to my room.

It was quite a basic hotel, but it was more than sufficient for an overnight stay for a touring cyclist. Having had the steak only a few hours before, I didn't need dinner, so I decided to have a little walk around the town. I bought some supplies from a small supermarket, then enjoyed a couple of beers in a backstreet bar by the river, watching a tired dad teach his excited son how to fish.

As I sat there staring into the distance over the river, relaxing and processing each element of the day I'd just enjoyed, the blue afternoon sky gently faded to grey and fat raindrops started to slowly fall. I tried to style it out for a minute before the rain got heavier, leaving me walking over the greasy floor in my slippery flip-flops like I had broom stick up my bottom, heading for some shelter underneath a small canopied area outside the bar.

The father also ran for cover with his son, then quickly popped to the bar to buy himself a beer and some crisps for his son. Then they sat, sheltering from the shower, chatting, and tidying up their fishing equipment.

If Carling did Best Cycling Days, today would be right up there, albeit with an Estrella to finish things Spanish-style.

101km for the day - 1,519km travelled.

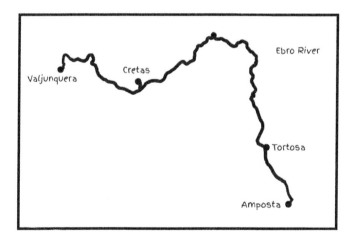

Day 19 - Amposta to Grau de Castelló

As I rounded the next corner of the dogleg, I had to wonder what the person who came up with six was thinking or how they measured it in the first place.

With just four cycling days to go, I decided that I wanted to hammer out a couple of big days to make the last two shorter and more enjoyable. I was still well on track and could change things if needed with my new (semi) flexible personality. So, with the extra distance in mind, today was going to be a challenge.

I was awake early and mingling with the workmen at the breakfast buffet as it opened. Different groups of work colleagues sat together quietly, preparing themselves, no doubt, for a hard day's graft. I sat alone, scoffing carbs and staring into the distance.

Overnight, Terence and the other bikes had been moved to the edge of the conference room, which now had rows of stackable chairs ready for what looked like a very boring presentation. Perhaps it was a compliance seminar for the workmen dragging out their pastries at the buffet upstairs. Or, it could have been a speed awareness course. It was that kind of hotel.

Packed and ready to go, I was out of the door by eight o'clock, and as I stood getting my bearings next to the river, I was taken aback by how windy it was this morning. As with much of my trip, luck was on my side; the wind was going in the same direction as me.

I followed the river, but only for one kilometre, where I finally said goodbye to the Ebra after four days of being my powerful blue companion, guiding me coastwards. As I continued southwards, the river would flow its final 25km east and into the Mediterranean at the Parc Natural del Delta de l'Ebre.

Leaving the town on the TV-3408, I soon found myself quickly hammering down a long, flat, straight road. Bashing out the first few kilometres of the day always felt good, and before long, I arrived at the marina at La Ràpita, where I stopped to look out over the wide blue blanket of the Mediterranean.

It was still only eight-thirty, and the road cleaners were out, busy clearing away yesterday's debris. A café owner was going through her morning ritual of unstacking chairs and laying out tables, preparing for passing trade in the beautiful setting - not a bad vista to have as a workplace. Like all of us and our daily surroundings, no matter how grand, she no doubt takes it for granted.

I didn't. It was all fresh and new to me, and I had just cycled from my house in England to the Mediterranean Sea, another landmark moment that sent my mind on a quick journey. Having thought about this ride for the best part of seven years, planning it for two, and now being here by the Med, it felt like such an achievement. Not that I'd ever admit that, of course. I'm British, after all.

I vocalised my deep thinking by repeating, 'The Mediterranean Sea. You've just cycled here, Craig! The Fucking Mediterranean Sea!'.

I sent a couple of messages and posted a short video to my social media channels, hoping people didn't think I was showing off, especially as they'd probably just be getting ready for work. I didn't want to be THAT prick. I'd been posting to Instagram, Facebook and LinkedIn, telling myself it was all for the fundraising, but deep down, I was enjoying the small amount of feedback I was getting from my videos, and there was also a part of the interaction that made me feel less alone.

Social media is a slippery slope, though, and I'd have to come straight back off the crack cocaine of Instagram as soon as I got back home. Either that, or surrender to the fact that I'd end up spending hours a week in a daze, mesmerised by videos of people tying knots, telling dad jokes (laughing at their own hilarity no matter how crap the joke is), and getting bombarded with adverts telling me how I could lose my middle-age belly with a workout that takes just five minutes a day.

Back on the bike and cycling along the flat N-340, I was making good speed. It was a busy road but also very dull, and I started wondering if my last few days would be like this, all the way to Benidorm. I could do boring for a few days, especially if the road was flat and the sun was shining, as long as it didn't stay this busy. I'd had enough adventurous days on the trip and saw this last section of the ride as my very own final day of the Tour De France, a procession.

I knew I had some hills coming up today, but overall, the landscape wasn't going to be challenging, gently undulating all the way to the day's destination, Castellón de la Plana, with some climbing sandwiched in the middle.

Finally, after 13km of the busy N-340, I veered off through Vinaròs, being popped out onto the Eurovelo 8 on the other side of the coastal town.

The Eurovelo network contains several guided cycle routes right across Europe. This particular one (number eight) travels from Cadiz in southern Spain, around the Mediterranean coast side of the country, across France and Italy, before heading all the way down the Adriatic coast to the southern tip of Greece and, strangely, across the sea to Cyprus.

After having ridden an hour or so along the main coast road, it was a very welcome change to be traffic-free. It was a warm morning, and here I was, cycling on beautiful country lanes with luscious vegetable fields to my right, abundant with colour and life, and the expanse of the sea to my left. Should I share another photo on the 'Gram'? No, stop it, Craig!

The minor back roads were less direct than the main road, with quite a few stops and turns at junctions. I was going forward, right, left, and sometimes slightly backward. I was still making good progress, though, as I hit the seaside stretch between the towns of Benicarló and Peniscola, where the route directed me onto a cycle path along the promenade.

Considering the time of year, it was lively along the front, and the SAGA crowd was taking full advantage of the clement weather and the cheap hotel prices on the Costas. After having had the road to myself for a few kilometres, I suddenly had to factor in how to navigate through people who don't necessarily move that quickly out of the way, or, indeed, realise what the large white-painted bike on one side of the pathway means.

Past the Castell de Peníscola on the peninsular, I continued out of the central tourist area and over a couple of hilly roads that hugged the rugged coastline tightly before I noticed that I seemed to be heading for a rocky outcrop ahead. This must be the 'lumpy' section, I thought.

Eyeing the top of the large, sharp hill in front of me, I saw that the ridge ran inland for quite a few kilometres. Would it be too much to expect a tunnel here? I feared it might be.

As I left the edge of town, the road suddenly became rougher, as if the road was going to end, and as I came out of a sharp bend to the left, I was confronted with the sight no cyclist wants to see - a steep incline sign up ahead. Six percent; I could do that, even with all the weight.

As I rounded the next corner of the dogleg, I had to wonder what the person who came up with six was thinking or how they measured it in the first place. Perhaps they worked it out the same way I did the height of a tree in Junior school, with a protractor and a measuring tape, lying flat on the floor. Maybe they just rolled a dice and realised six was the highest number they could get to. A few minutes later, I was off the bike, leaning in and slowly pushing Terence up the gradient, looking at my bike computer, which showed it as 15%.

At the top of the steepest part of the incline, just to add some extra fun, the rough tarmac stopped abruptly. There was a track ahead - incredibly rough, with gaping holes and clusters of large stones. So much for my easy day!

As I neared the top of the sharp incline and the track started to level out, I got back on Terence and struggled up the rest of the hill as he bounced around, rattling in confusion. It wasn't a long hill, so we'd just have to grin and bear it and laugh about it later.

The apex finally came, and I stopped to take in the view and get some life back into my wobbling arms and legs. The panorama was stunning, well worth the effort, as I looked back down and across to the town I'd cycled through less than half an hour before.

As I turned to look the other way at what was to come, I saw a steep downhill, followed by no foreseeable life: No towns, no roads - just a forest, more hills, and a small track directly in front of me with a few hikers and mountain bikers. This was looking ominous.

It was time to consult Google Maps. I was being guided through the Parc Natural de la Serra d'Irta - 12,000 hectares of protected land that runs alongside the d'Irta Marine Reserve. For me, that translated to very challenging terrain for 20km, complete with a couple of cheeky steep climbs thrown in for good measure. I spent most of the time holding my breath waiting for a spoke to go ping.

It was soul-destroying. My average speed came right down with the constant jolts and wheel spins that sapped my energy. In my head, my plans for the day were changing from a 110km ride to eighty or ninety. It wouldn't be the end of the world; I just had to concentrate on getting through the park and back onto the roads.

It didn't help that I was getting passed constantly by people on electric bikes - many on high-spec mountain bikes with suspension, dressed in full Lycra, and, dare I say it, much younger than me. 'Come on, Terence, keep going. We'll show these losers what a proper cyclist is!'

The views helped, and I had to keep reminding myself to man up and enjoy the moment. That if I kept the sea to the left, Benidorm would appear in three more days. Just keep peddling, Craig.

Eventually, after nearly an hour and a half, which felt more like four hours, I reached tarmac again as the road hit the very edge of the first town back into civilisation. I felt relieved, but not as much as Terence. I'd had to stop during the off-roading for a quick repair after one of the panniers had come away from the frame from the constant jolting. We'd both been through the wringer, and all I wanted now were some boring roads, please.

We'd made it in one piece, though, and I cycled down from the hilly outskirts into another holiday spot - Alcossebre - with more old people eating ice cream.

By now, it was one o'clock, and having lost time cycling through the national park, I didn't want to stop for a sit-down lunch and take up valuable time. Pausing at a small supermarket - the type you get at a holiday spot which seems to sell everything from fresh bread to inflatable unicorns - I ransacked the shelves, bypassing the suncream and lilos and opting for ice cream, Coke and one of the best pastries I've ever had (although a tough morning of cycling may have skewed that rating).

Still on the Eurovelo 8, I wondered what would happen to someone on a less robust travelling bike than Terence following the cycle route in ignorant bliss. I bet a few people have come unstuck there in the past. Or, just maybe, they pay more attention than I do when planning their routes and end up going around it.

Back on smoother roads, I was once again chipping away at the distance, cycling through half-empty holiday spot after very-empty holiday spot. I was back on track and moving further and further southwards with the wind gently pushing me along. Between towns, I was on quiet back roads and even managed to overtake groups of older people on electric bikes, my midday adventure now well and truly behind me.

And then, as if someone flicked a switch in the sky, my lovely tailwind became a headwind, and it all became much more of a struggle. Scores of pensioners passed me, casually peddling along in slow motion with the help of their motors, looking on at me smugly.

Every evening on this trip, when I planned my route for the next day, I had a rough idea of where I wanted to finish or at least head for. Tonight's destination was the city of Castellón de la Plana, six kilometres inland. As the afternoon wore on and I got closer, I started to head away from the coast and up towards the city. Then, for some reason, I stopped dead in my tracks. I wanted to re-think things.

I knew that, in general, I was following the coast all the way down to Benidorm, so if I headed inland, I'd only need to come back down to the sea from the city again tomorrow morning to carry on. I also didn't fancy a climb inland, not that it was huge. So, I thought, why not just stay on the coast road and look for a hotel?

I quickly searched online and found vacancies in Grau de Castelló, ten kilometres further along the road I'd just left. The ride would be flat, if not a little windy, and I'd knock five unnecessary kilometres from my day. I was just about to book but, after yesterday's debacle, I decided to wing it and just arrive without a room and see if I could book in at the front desk. Jesus, who was this man? Craig 'I need to have it all planned out' Killick was winging it, once again!

Ten windy kilometres later, I came to a halt outside a stumpy, two-story building next to the sea. The Hotel Costa Azahar wasn't in a bustling tourist area, but there was a small fast-food restaurant downstairs, so everything I needed was right here. It reminded me of the type of hotel you'd land at on a cheap package holiday.

In my twenties, I went on a couple of package tours and always used to panic during the game of hotel roulette on the coach. As if being met by an overly enthusiastic clipboard-carrying rep at the airport wasn't bad enough, you had to endure the same rep forty minutes later, standing at the front of the coach with a microphone in their hand, trying to whip up an ounce of excitement from fifty people who have just flown through the night. Then the game would start, as the coach pulled up at nice hotel after nice hotel, with names called and families disembarking. Invariably, you would be stuck at the back of the coach with a few other small groups as it pulled up next to a shithole of a hotel, praying your name wouldn't be called. It never ended well. 'You pay your money, you takes your choice'. Ah, the joys of being tight with the holiday budget in the travel agents so you can keep your cash for spending in a sweaty bar each night, only to be rejected by holidaying girls from all over the world, rather than just the usual ones from home.

The Hotel Costa Azahar: I think this would be full of families getting off during the middle of the coach drop, wives looking to husbands for nods of approval on a choice made at the travel agents on a wet January morning.

I parked Terence out the front and walked in, unsure what to expect or, indeed, what to say. Using my limited Spanish, I explained to the young lady behind the counter that I didn't have a booking but could see online that they had vacancies. I thought I was doing them a favour by cutting out the website commission, but it looked like they wanted to charge me as much as they could. I held my phone, showing her the listing and got a curt nod in return.

She then held up her phone, using Google translate, asking me something about being married. 'What's it got to do with you?' I thought. Then, an older man beside her explained she was asking if I wanted a single or double bed, to which I replied large, of course. 'That's an extra €15, yes,' he replied in his thick Spanish accent. 'Small bed it is, then,' I said, wondering if I should have just stuck to the booking.com.

With Terence locked away in a cupboard and me settling into my twin room, I opened the patio door to reveal a balcony pretty much on the beach. It was gorgeous. I say 'pretty much' on the beach because right below me was the outdoor seating area for the burger bar, complete with a kid's party taking place.

The contrast in hotels each night on my trip, especially over the past few days, was now complete. I had stayed in so many different places over the past couple of weeks, and this hotel was my first tourist experience. It made me realise how far I'd travelled. Even the noise of the children laughing and shouting at each other was acceptable in the background as I showered, stretched, hung up my shower-fresh clothes to dry and got changed.

With no other restaurants nearby - it was quite an industrial area, considering it was right near an expansive beach - I headed down to the burger bar, which pleasingly sold beer alongside its soft drink selection. I ate my burger, looking out over the large beach and out to sea, the party of screaming kids thankfully gone now.

The evening was still young, and I needed to stock up on a few things, so I walked to the closest supermarket, which was two kilometres away - just what I needed after a day of cycling. Then, I headed back to my room and sat on my balcony, with the quiet chattering of the late-night diners below me.

As I worked on my laptop, sipping an ice-cold beer, I sat contented, watching the last of the day's sun throw long shadows across the beach. I was getting close.

111km for the day - 1,630km travelled.

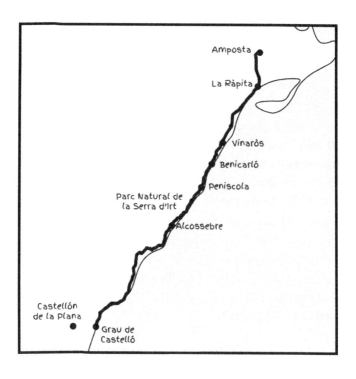

Amposta

La Ràpita

Vinaròs

Benicarló

Peníscola

Parc Natural de
la Serra d'Irt

Alcossebre

Castellón
de la Plana

Grau de
Castelló

Day 20 - Grau de Castelló to Cullera

All I really wanted to do was get in some serious distance. And I did, just shy of 116km.

After completing my morning routine of making ham and cream cheese baguettes over the bathroom sink with my pen knife, I went to the beach to enjoy the early morning sun. I had half an hour to kill while I waited for the hotel reception to open so that I could retrieve Terence.

The sun was low over the sea, surrounded by a bright white halo. The horizon, still trying to shake off the night, was a delicious deep orange as it hit the water, fading up through yellow to the beautiful bright blue sky above and beyond. As I walked towards the water, cold sand forcing its way between my toes, I felt like a child, listening to the windless waves gently lapping against the shore and walking along the beach as far as I could with my eyes closed until I panicked. The sound of the sea never gets boring, however old I get.

I was feeling tired. Maybe my body knew the end of the ride was just three days away and was preparing itself. The fact that it manifested as fatigue wasn't particularly helpful right now, mind, with my plans for a big day ahead.

And so it was, as I set off for the morning, cycling past the supermarket I'd been to the night before, wondering why I hadn't just ridden and saved myself a sweaty hour and a half of walking.

The first twenty kilometres of the morning were challenging. Cycling inland to Almassora, on the outskirts of Castellón de la Plana, before heading south on the CV-18, the roads were plain; no off-roading like yesterday. As ever, I was glad to get some distance in early. The excitement of seeing the sea had passed, and my legs were aching with every turn of the pedal. At times like this, I knew it was just a case of grinning and bearing it and hoping that the fatigue would soon pass. And that's what I did, perhaps without the grinning part.

Across a mixture of cycle paths that ran alongside busy roads, hard shoulders next to busy roads, and cycling on the busy roads themselves, mixing it up with the endless stream of lorries and cars, I carried on south, through busy towns like Sagunto, completely bypassing any sights it had to offer.

By lunchtime, the roadways were getting broader and busier as I entered the outlying areas of Valencia. The orange groves that lined my way were replaced with trading estates, and vans and lorries collecting and delivering their loads became my road-mates. There was roundabout after roundabout after roundabout as arterial roads connected the commercial hub.

As lunchtime approached, I stopped to eat my bathroom baguette. As per my usual modus operandi, this wasn't in a beautiful park setting or by a river, but next to a large bin behind a commercial unit just off the main road. Needs must. It made it very easy to get rid of all my rubbish without moving a muscle.

Carbed up and back on the bike, the roads continued into the city until south of Albalat dels Sorells. I had cycled 67km and was pleased to finally come off the busy main roads and onto the Via Xurra, a mixed-use path for cyclists and hikers which took me over the Carraixet Ravine and into the town of Alboraya, where I once again found myself back on roads, thankfully much quieter than earlier in the day.

This continued until I hit a vast multi-junction roundabout, with the V-21 running underneath and the Torre Miramar proudly sitting in the centre. On a bike, there was no way I was going over it, but luckily, the crossings for walkers and cyclists allowed me to get around to the other side - albeit a bit stop-starty - constantly waiting for green lights to appear. Side roads next to the main boulevards on the other side of the roundabout allowed me to continue my journey into the heart of Valencia without contending with the mass of cars.

Constant traffic light stops meant I was making slow progress, but I eventually made my way down to the Avenue d'Aragó, back on the main road and weaving through the heavy traffic on the four-lane roadway and across the Pont d'Aragó.

Directly after crossing the bridge, I was off the road, breathing a huge sigh of relief as I descended a short, sharp ramp down to the Jardín del Turia below.

My memory suddenly kicked in like a movie flashback as Richard Ayoade pottered through this very same park on his Travel Man programme, explaining to his companion how the park came to be.

The course of the River Turia - which used to run through the heart of Valencia and into the sea until a devastating flood in 1957 - had been diverted south of the city to prevent the devastation from happening again. This had left nine kilometres of dry river bed, which was converted into a luscious parkway for the people of the city, and I was cycling right through it now. I love it when my memory actually works. Now, what was I saying again?

The long and winding city centre park seemed like a boundless oasis, a perfect centrepiece to the urban jungle above. I dodged people on rental bikes and swerved to miss electric scooter crews and large families with errant children. They were getting on my nerves. Don't get me wrong, I love a City Break as much as the next man - as long as that man is someone who wants to be a tourist but doesn't want any other tourists to be there at the same time as him.

After a kilometre of gentle cycling and weaving, I was hit with the futuristic combination of the Queen Sofia Palace of Arts, the Hemisfèric, the Museu de les Ciències Príncipe Felipe, the Ciudad de las Artes y las Ciencias and the L'Àgora. If I were, in fact, in Valencia on a city break, I could have spent half a day on a picnic blanket just looking at the architecture of this collection of buildings. But I wasn't. I was simply itching to crack on and get out of the city. I still had 40km to go before reaching my destination for the day, Cullera.

And so I did. I edged my way through the crowds, tutting with every peddle stroke, usually at the latest idiot to wobble on their hire bike in front of me. Then, finally, out the other side, onto a cycle path away from the hordes, cycling south of the city and over a large bridge crossing the revised passage of the river Turia.

The transition from city to countryside to the south was immediate, and I was soon back on small country roads riding into the Parc Natural dl'Albuferara. The traffic was busy at points as I rode through El Perellonet, El Perelló and Les Palmeres, and the afternoon weather was sweltering. But I was enjoying the flat terrain, especially after stopping at a garage to top up on water and buy a giant ice cream to keep me going.

Similarly to yesterday, the southerly wind had become northerly during the afternoon, turning against me. Still, despite the extra challenge, my aching legs from first thing this morning were a distant memory as I powered on.

As I continued south, my surroundings offered a sharp contrast depending on which way I looked, with hotels and holiday properties on my left towards the sea and large, old, plastic greenhouses on my right - hundreds of them, all looking somewhat dilapidated.

My destination, the town of Cullera, moved closer and closer. It sounded lovely, especially saying it out loud with the rolling double-L - 'Cuyera'. In my head, it would be a small town, perhaps with a fishing port and a couple of excellent seafood restaurants, one of which I would dine in tonight. I'd pinpointed the Sicania Hotel as a place to stay. It was in the far north of the town and, once again, was flying by the seat of my pants with no booking.

As I got closer to the town, I entered the hotel address into Google Maps to guide me in. My original route to the generic centre of town suddenly became one kilometre shorter but now involved much more climbing as I headed east around the cape rather than inland to miss the outcrop, sitting dead in the centre between me and the town. The hill didn't make me downhearted as they so often do; I was nearly there. I stuck Terence in a low gear, dug in and slowly rose up the steep incline and round the final bend by the sea's edge to be confronted with a vision of the town.

Cullera wasn't the small fishing village I'd envisaged, whether you said it out loud or not. It was a mini-Benidorm with high-rise blocks as far as the eye could see.

I pulled up to the Hotel Sicania and sat on my bike for a few minutes, staring and wondering if I really wanted to stay there. It was on the edge of town and looked lifeless. But, with my newfound status as a travelling maverick and no booking as of yet, I had options. The option I took was to get back in the saddle and cycle down to the centre of town to see what else was available.

Onto the promenade, the beach was expansive, sandy and stunning - the juxtaposition of why it was currently dwarfed by high-rise blocks that had risen to deal with the fruitful tourism that comes with such a glorious coastline. But, right now, both the beach and the promenade were deserted as I cycled into the strengthening wind blowing hard across the sand and into my face.

I paused as I got closer to what I thought was the centre of town to check on booking.com. After a minute of searching, I found a hotel; aptly named the Cullera Holiday Hotel.

Cycling up to it, this was by far the poshest hotel I'd visited on my trip. I parked Terence in the covered car drop-off area and walked through the large glass doors into the air-conditioned foyer, looking very much out of place with my shabby cycling clothes and still wearing my helmet and gloves.

I said Hola, ready to knock them bandy with my travelling cyclist routine. I explained to the smiling receptionist that I didn't have a room but had seen on the website that they had vacancies, to which she replied positively with a price which was €30 more expensive than the website was showing. She couldn't, or wouldn't, budge and gave me an excellent impression of a French Waiter, complete with a Gaelic shrug. This was not going well, despite my best intentions.

Being British, being a man, and being me, I retreated to my phone to book through the App, which once again decided to play silly buggers when I needed it most. So, I spent ten minutes faffing around, unpacking my laptop and booking a room online so that I could walk back up to the reception and tell them I had a booking.

After waiting a minute for the confirmation to come through their system, she finally acknowledged the email with a smile, as if I'd just walked in through the door as a new customer. What a funny world we live in.

'Your English is very good', I chanced. Once again, it worked a treat, and we soon became best buddies. By the time she handed over my room key, I'd heard the story of how she'd spent time working at a hotel in London when she was much younger. 'You don't look old enough!' I lied sincerely.

At this point, I was still trying to figure out what would be happening with Terence, but the best response I could muster when I asked was, 'Yes, it is all fine.' It ended up being more than fine.

Having pushed Terence into the reception through the large glass front door, we were led through ground floor corridors and past 'the gym on your left if you wanted to work out.' Um, no thanks.

Then, the door of a special room was unlocked. It was a dedicated bike room. It was clean and secure, with locks for several bikes on the wall. It had tools and pumps and even a wash sink. 'We've landed on our wheels here, Terence,' I said, getting some funny looks from my new receptionist friend as I parked him up for the night.

Showered and changed, and having already checked out the sea view from my balcony, I walked back out and down towards the beach again to find somewhere to eat along the promenade.

The wind had picked up even more, and the few people wandering around earlier had obviously retreated to their warm, windless bedrooms back at their hotels, probably on a floor with double digits, and making the most of their sea views between the towering concrete obstructions.

I walked in the rough direction where I thought the shops and restaurants would be - there weren't any. Although this place was undoubtedly a bustling resort in the summer, on this windy evening in early May, the restaurants I passed were all still locked up, with tables and chairs stacked high inside. It must be a weird way to work; closed for half the year, then, no doubt, working all the hours you could during the summer to make up the money.

I passed a Burger King. Surely this would not be my evening's bounty? I gambled on finding something better; it wasn't Sunday after all; something must be open!

After a few hundred metres more, some shops appeared in a square, so I walked in from the beach a couple of blocks and came across the centre of town, stumbling across a small restaurant on the side of a street. There was a mixture of ageing tourists in summer wear, grabbing an early evening meal, and tables with groups of locals sipping drinks, dressed like it was the middle of winter. I was wearing shorts and a T-shirt - say no more.

It's funny looking back on days like this because they end up just being a lot of cycling with two or three key memories peppered in, which usually have nothing to do with cycling. I've wanted a weekend in Valencia for as long as I can remember. I may well return one day. But that is much easier to do when you've just hopped on a plane for an hour and a half for a weekend rather than in the middle of a full day of cycling. It felt a little haze-like being there and ended up being less than one hour of my day. I also couldn't wait to leave the city by the time I hit the centre.

Perhaps, as I've mentioned before, like so many things we think about, the thought of the thing is better than the reality when it happens. Especially in this case, when the circumstances aren't entirely aligned. Today, tourists were getting on my nerves. But I have been that annoying tourist many times in my life and have probably walked in front of a travelling cyclist more than once and not even noticed.

I had completed the two long days of cycling down the coast I'd wanted to. All I had left was a short run down to Denia tomorrow, where I would meet Lorraine and another friend, Matthew, who had come out a day early for my grand arrival in Benidorm. We had planned to meet for lunch before they headed to the villa, and I spent my last night in a hotel.

Part of me was glad that the ride would soon be over. But realising that my adventure - a big part of my life for the past two years - was ending was bringing up a weird mix of emotions I would need to process.

For now, I'd done the hard work. I could relax with my beer and schnitzel. I just needed to remember to soak up the final two days of the adventure.

116km for the day - 1,746km travelled.

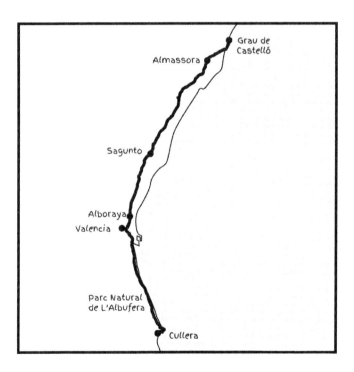

Day 21 - Cullera to Javea

If you look straight ahead and to the right a bit, you'll see a big buffoon-looking bloke in a pink T-shirt waving like an idiot. Yes... That's me.

I woke up excited. I was going to see friendly faces today. Having been in the same routine for three weeks, except for one day off in Bordeaux nearly two weeks ago, it felt surreal to know there was only one more hotel stop.

I'd been replaying the finish in my head: Being met in Benidorm on the esplanade outside a rowdy bar, crying as I saw Lorraine, the emotion of three weeks on my own suddenly released. This mind journey was becoming a dangerous game, and I kept welling up just at the thought. Of course, I should know better about imagined thoughts of future events. After all, I was leaning on the balcony rail of my sixth-floor room, staring out over the 'fishing village' I had imagined I'd be staying in yesterday.

I decided to splash out and pay €11 to enjoy the buffet breakfast before I left for a day of cycling. There was a fantastic array of food available, and I'd like to say I made the most of the variety. But I ate exactly the same as I had every morning on this trip when faced with a buffet, albeit much better quality than I was used to.

The restaurant area was incredibly busy, with a coachload of Japanese tourists hurriedly finishing their morning meals before scurrying away to get their cases and head out on the next leg of their journey. The more casual of them were still pouring coffee. At the same time, from the basement level restaurant, I could see the legs of the more eager travellers as they rolled their suitcases towards the idling coach outside.

I sat in wonder at what kind of trip it must be that they were on. Was there really a travel agent in downtown Kyoto selling coach trips down the Costas in Spain to unsuspecting Japanese tourists? No offence to the Costa Blanca, but it's not exactly Athens, Paris or Vienna, is it? Or Machu Picchu. Maybe later today, they'll be driving slowly through the centre of Benidorm with the rep at the front of the coach on a microphone, 'And on your left, you will see a special type of British weekend tourist. Not so rare in these parts, this one. You can tell they are British by their red arms and white bodies and the tribal markings on their calf muscles of three lions.' Cameras would click away, and they'd all be looking at each other, nodding and murmuring like only Japanese tourists can, bonding over yet more proof of their fantastic choice of holiday.

After retrieving Terence from his overnight suite, we rolled out of the foyer and gently down the slope outside the hotel, turning south towards the centre of town, where I'd eaten the night before. Today was a short day, and I had my lunch date in Denia to look forward to, which was only a flat 57 kilometres away.

The sun was shining, and so was my mood as as I left the built-up area of Cullera and out over the River Júcar, to be met with smooth, quiet lanes and back on another section of the Eurovelo 8.

It was an uneventful morning of gentle cycling through the town of Gandia, where the countryside stopped and was replaced with what seemed like a string of urbanizaciones, interspersed with restaurants and shops. Through Oliva and Molinell, it wasn't long before I hit the outskirts of Denia. I'd been here on holiday eight years ago but struggled to recognise the area where I'd stayed, even though I must have passed it at some point. Even as I hit the middle of the town, no bells rang in my memory. Eight years was obviously a long time in the town's development, or, more likely, the loss of memory cells in my head.

I stopped near the marina and sat under a tree in the hot midday sun, popping off a message to my lunch buddies to see how they were getting on. They were still en route from the airport. Having taken an early flight, no doubt with all the dawn revellers excitedly rinsing Gatwick Wetherspoons of alcohol, they had collected their car and were not too far away.

Rather than stay sat on a wall, I headed to the far side of the marina out onto the sizeable man-made sea barrier, which housed bars, restaurants and nautical shops. A 'happy-go-lucky' waitress reluctantly allowed me to sit in one of the empty restaurants so that I could have a drink.

Terence was banished to the other side of the esplanade by my jolly new friend so that he wouldn't get in the way of the bustling tourists, of which there were none. I parked him next to the railings and the expensive boats bobbing around in the sheltered bay and returned to relax and wait. To be fair, there are worse places to be banished to.

Having not seen Lorraine since Bordeaux, I was excited to see her. We'd Facetimed most days, but it's not the same. I was looking forward to a hug and some human contact. With my Coke to one side, along with the obligatory bowl of nuts, I had my laptop out, struggling to get an internet connection to plan my next move for the day. I had intended to stop here in Denia, but it seemed silly with it still being so early, and I would have plenty of time left in the day, even after a lengthy lunch. I decided that I'd carry on later. It would be good to knock some kilometres off, leaving me a more leisurely morning to Benidorm. Besides, as I'd had an easy morning this morning and would be fuelled after my meal, I could also get two hundred metres of climbing out of the way around the Montgó Massif, which sits between Denia and Javea.

Waiting an age for pages to load with my intermittent connection, I painstakingly searched booking.com so that I could relax in the knowledge that I was sorted for the evening. Eventually, as my second Coke arrived, I finally got confirmation on a room at the Hotel Villa Naranjos at Playa del Arenal, Jávea. Closing my laptop, I felt content and relaxed. And then my phone rang.

'We're here!' came Lorraine's excited voice.

'Did you park where I said? I sent you a message with a pin for a car park. I am near there, by the far side of the marina, in a café, having a drink'.

'I don't know; we just followed the signs to some parking. We're by some trees!'

'Okay, I'll send you a pin to show you where I am now.'

The conversation continued like this for a minute or two, with me trying to explain that it didn't matter to me where they were if I had sent them my location. It wasn't worth us both moving, and I had a Coke on the go in a beautiful marina-side café. Besides, even with my view of the boats gently bobbing on the sea, I could see about a million trees. Just as I was trying to explain this for the third time to my very excited listener, I saw them both walking towards me in the distance.

'If you look straight ahead and to the right a bit, you'll see a big buffoon-looking bloke in a pink T-shirt waving like an idiot. Yes… That's me… Yes, him… Yes. That's me… See you in a minute!'

It was worth the wait, and I can't remember the last time I enjoyed such an embrace, even though, in the corner of my eye, my friend Matthew was casually waiting, trying not to feel awkward. I gave him a hug for good measure.

Despite the fact we'd not seen each other for a long time, we did what most people do and started chatting about mundane stuff within minutes. It was nice. I couldn't comprehend, let alone translate my experience yet, to answer any questions, so I didn't even try. To their credit, they didn't push me.

After a drink, we slowly walked back around the marina and down the street that ran parallel to the water's edge, finding a small square set back from the road with a row of restaurants that looked ideal for three English tourists. It was time to have a beer and order far too many tapas. (You know you've ordered too much when you're more than full up, and there are still three dishes to come.)

It was great catching up, speaking English, and having a conversation; it was so relaxing and in complete contrast to the simple, stilted exchanges I'd had over the past couple of weeks, and I realised just how much I'd missed chatting with friends. Just one more night of solitude left.

After a couple of hours of chatting and eating, and repeating the phrase, 'Urgh, I think I've eaten too much' a few times, it was time to say our goodbyes. Luckily, it would be less than 24 hours until I would see them again, so it wasn't a heavy farewell, more of a see you later.

Having seen Lorraine in the flesh, the idea of crying when I saw her in Benidorm had disappeared. But as I cycled off, the awareness that the end of the ride was rearing its head brought up a mix of emotions: excitement, sadness, and pride. Despite my lunchtime deadly sin of gluttony, pride is not something I particularly feel ever, unless it's about someone else. And despite it rearing its head, albeit in a positive way, it's not an emotion I would be sharing any time soon. So, if we could keep that one to ourselves, I'd be grateful.

Luckily, I had a big hill to concentrate on to take my mind off it.

The road between Denia and Jávea climbs around the peak of Montgó Massif, a 753m mountain that marks the last spur on the Cordillera Prebética Mountain Range. Although I'd only be climbing a third of that height over five of the remaining fourteen kilometres, it would still be a challenge, especially, as with my other days along the coast, I was now battling my customary afternoon headwind and also carrying a large belly full of food.

An issue appeared immediately as I headed out of Denia towards the one road that joined the two towns over the pass. My passage was blocked by roadworks.

Remaining calm and heading inland, I could see an alternative route on my computer and hoped the road would be open if I joined it further up after a little detour; otherwise, it looked like I'd have to go right around the other side of the mountain.

A side road took me up a steep incline into an area of houses, and, luckily, after a few left and rights, and with just enough breath left to keep the pedals turning in the lowest gear, I popped back out on the main road further up the hill, which was now quiet with very little traffic and, more importantly, open.

Continuing up, and after climbing fifty metres in less than a kilometre, I was glad of the respite as the road flattened, then descended slightly over the first, smaller hill - an entrée, if you will. Because as I rounded the corner, I could see what was coming and where I was heading. And it was mainly up. Head down, I just kept peddling in my lowest gear, slowly inching up the hill.

The following thirty-five minutes and three and a half kilometres saw me gradually climb the final two hundred metres, rounding the switchbacks before reaching the open, shallower final rise, the wind now battering me across the open ridge.

With a sheer drop on one side of me and rocks on the other, there were no hard shoulders on either side, and I had to stop on the road a couple of times to rest and keep my fingers crossed that no traffic would come. It was a relief when the road finally flattened at the top.

I pulled into a small gravel car park to catch my breath and grab a drink, watching the hikers returning to their cars from their walks, celebrating their achievements quietly and knowingly with each other as they changed out of their boots.

Then, it was time for the descent.

With no cars on my side of the road, I effortlessly glided down into the town, enjoying the sweeping hill, the long, soft turns, and the view of the bay below. As I hit the edge of Javea with one sharp final switchback - complete with a lorry coming the other way so that I couldn't fully enjoy it - I entered the town, turning left onto busy roads towards the sea and along the front for the final four kilometres to the tourist area of Playa del Arenal.

Hotel Villa Naranjos was a holiday hotel, and there were, as you'd expect, people there on holiday. My room was fine for one night, but I'm not sure I could have done a week here, or even a long weekend. It suits some folk, though, and I watched as a couple walked their red torsos back to their rooms, struggling with cases of beer under their arms. Terence was placed in a poorly locked shed, which luckily had some railings in, so I could secure him for the night with a tiny bit of reassurance that he'd still be there in the morning when I went to collect him.

During my usual evening routine of showering, the last on my trip, I passed on cleaning clothes, what with only one half day of cycling left. Refreshed, I headed down to the promenade, where I found myself well and truly with the tourists, many of whom were British.

After my rather large lunch earlier, I didn't feel the need for food, so I found a bar and took advantage of the 'happy hour' prices, sipping on a weak Gin and Tonic or two. Despite being on my own, I enjoyed sitting there for a couple of hours, staring out over the beach. As the late afternoon gradually became early evening, it was still bustling with end-of-day tanners and a local gymnastics class with youngsters flinging themselves around on the sand. What must they make of the tourists, I wondered.

I also had no choice but to listen in on two couples sitting around the table next to me. They seemed to be taking even more advantage of 'happy hour' than me, and were acting out what seemed like an Alan Bennett play, helped along with their ageing stereotypical northern dialogue. Reminded of the phrase you often hear, 'you couldn't write this', I really wish I'd had a notebook and pen.

'Susan, our neighbour, or was it her sister? Oo, I think it might have been her sister… What's her name again? Gina. Georgia, Janet… Oh, never mind… Yes, she had that… Ended up in hospital for two weeks, she did.'

'Yes, our Brian's good at walking. Well, he's a postman, you see. When he gets going, he really gets some momento going.'

I stifled my chuckles.

Between them on my left and the old couple on my right, debating for half an hour over one Pinacolada between them whether they should go back to the room and sit on the balcony, I was entertained. To be honest, I bloody loved it.

I was back in my room, sitting at my computer, ready to edit my last daily video, when a message from my friend Ian (my Bordeaux cycling companion who was busy dodging sniper bullets) popped up on my computer asking me if I had a good Internet connection. It was a strange question, but I typed yes and pressed send.

Two minutes later, I pressed play on a video he'd sent me, my eyes already weeping as Spanish music started playing. I knew what was coming, and it started with an image of Ian and Lorraine driving over a footbridge in Basingstoke on mobility scooters.

One after another, messages with good wishes and congratulations flowed. From my daughters, my grandchildren, my family, friends and colleagues. It was overwhelming as I sat in my hotel room sobbing like a child.

I saw this challenge as something any healthy, able-bodied person could do if they wanted to. I genuinely believe that. It's not easy, but it's certainly not out of reach. But, to sit here in a hotel room and realise that there are people out there cheering you on, well, it really hit a nerve.

I've not had Cancer, so I have absolutely no idea what it must feel like to get a diagnosis and the fear that comes with it. The Pink Place helps people like that. It's not a big charity, and it doesn't have a vast budget or teams of people employed to raise money. With an annual income in the region of £120,000, I had reached over £15,000 doing this ride and knew what a difference this money would make to the charity and the people who rely on it.

Sometimes (every time), you simply have to play to your strengths. I can ride a bike, and I can do marketing and I had managed to turn that into something special.

Yes, I was getting the plaudits, but I couldn't have done it on my own, and, for the rest of my life, I will never forget the generosity of the people who put their money where their mouth was to support me, along with those that had also supported me on a much more personal level, Ian included. When people congratulate me on doing this challenge, I will always be quick to remind them that it was very much a team effort and I couldn't have done it on my own.

And, after just one more sleep, it would all be over.

72km for the day - 1,818km travelled.

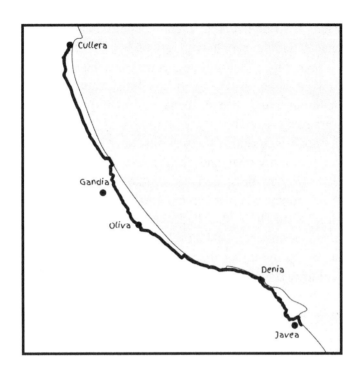

Day 22 - Jávea to Benidorm

And then, I heard the cowbells.

I had been wondering about the last day of my ride for some time now - how I would feel at the end, seeing good friends and my partner standing there at the finish line, and all the emotions that would go with finally completing this journey of a lifetime. Whiling away hours cycling, I'd run through the scenario in my head so many times, but of course, as I've said before, the reality ended up being nothing like any of the countless movie versions I'd replayed on the journey.

The breakfast buffet at the Hotel Villa Naranjos was everything I'd imagined it would be. As I walked out of the lift into the reception at 7:28am, naïvely thinking I'd be the only person there, I was welcomed by a throng of people milling around, eagerly waiting for the doors of the restaurant to open at seven-thirty.

Then we were off. It was like a race. The more established patrons steamed in, heading to their favourite tables, throwing down their room keys before turning back in one smooth single motion - like an Olympic swimmer doing a tumble turn -

straight to the central buffet to fill their plates. It was like flies around shit.

Talking of shit, the food was awful. The bread was hard, the tasteless butter was runny, and the meats - and I use the term lightly so you know which ballpark we are in - looked like the sort of toy meats children have in a play kitchen set - bright and plastic. The coffee, a staple I relied on each morning like a hit of drugs, was so weak I could easily see the bottom of the cup. The orange juice was like watery squash.

It didn't stop some of my fellow guests, though, piling their plates up to the ceiling and doing nothing to conceal the fact they were taking things for lunch, liberally walking around filling bags with bread, cakes and fruit like a contestant on Supermarket Sweep. At least I had the decency to pretend I was making a roll to eat for my breakfast before wrapping it in a napkin and hiding it in my pocket.

It was like some sort of competition as couples and pairs of friends from all European nations competed to make the tallest mountains of food on their plates. If they had been wearing funny outfits, it could well have been a round on It's A Knockout.

If you are too young to remember It's a Knockout, look it up on YouTube. That way, next time your parents or grandparents talk about the good old days and how 'we only had three or four TV channels, but it was more than good enough, not like you youngsters on your phones all the time', you can remind them how rubbish entertainment actually was back then. I just watched a few minutes of it online, and all I can say is thank heavens to Tim Berners-Lee for deciding he needed some sort of very big computer network.

To be fair, I have nostalgic memories of the programme. For some reason, it often had European nations competing against each other, with participants having to wear a range of big, silly costumes to undertake ridiculous tasks, usually while struggling to stand up. But the funniest part was when one of the commentators, Stuart Hall, started laughing uncontrollably - perhaps trying to explain which person dressed as a penguin falling over on a slippery revolving platform trying to fill a bucket of water was winning. The shine came off that one, though. He would later progress to being a convicted paedophile. 'Ah yes, you're right; me being on my phone is so much worse than the good old days, Dad.'

Having watched England dominate the buffet round, with not a laughing sex offender in sight (that I knew of), I headed back to my room, somewhat disappointed that I hadn't had my usual four cups of strong coffee. It was time to pack my pannier bags for the last time.

Terence had enjoyed his night in the lockup outside, and I treated him to one last oil and rub down as we prepared for our last fifty kilometres of the trip together, rolling out of the hotel car park just after eight o'clock.

I was aiming to finish along the promenade in Benidorm around lunchtime, and although the route was going to be a lot of ups and downs along the coast road, I was very much looking forward to my final day of cycling.

I was riding with a smile on my face as I crisscrossed Jávea and made my way southwards. The roads were busy, but I had plenty of wide, hard shoulders to take advantage of, except for Benitachell, which had the joyful combination of a steep, narrow road with no hard shoulder, full of traffic. This after having already climbed 150 metres in the lead-up to the town and flagging.

Then, it was a sharp left at the top, followed by a glorious sweeping road for five kilometres back down, wiping out the altitude in one fell swoop to the coastal town of Moraira as I got my breath back.

I was making good time and enjoying the day, with any sadness of finishing my adventure put to bed by the thought of, well, finishing. Things are what they are when they are. Then they are not.

Out of Moraira, I continued along the coastal road. Twists, turns, ups and downs, it was a great road to cycle. As I mooched along, plenty of other cyclists passed by enjoying the morning's weather, including some very large pelotons with lorries and cars patiently stacked behind them. I'm not sure there would be quite the same dynamic on an English road, that's for sure.

The immense outcrop of the Parc Natural del Penyal d'Ifac loomed before me. It would have looked lovely if it wasn't for the monstrosity of the Calpe skyline right next to it, with its large dominating high-rises offering a precursor to Benidorm.

When I reached the town, I couldn't ride through it quickly enough, apart from a quick pause to look at the flamingos feeding in the salt lake at Las Salinas, almost in the centre of the town. Then, it was out of the flat valley, which meant more rolling hills and my second taxing climb of the day. Only 125 metres this time, but having spent 22 days on the bike, my legs, which had become stronger and stronger, managed it slowly, but very steadily.

Back on the main coastal road again, with thirty kilometres already under my belt and the end within touching distance, I saw my first sign for Benidorm - just nineteen kilometres away. I had to stop to get a photo.

Then, a few minutes later, near the small town of Pueblo Mascarat, I exited a small tunnel around the edge of the coastline. There she was in the distance, simmering in the sunlight - Benidorm.

After cycling around 1,850 kilometres with just fifteen to go, barring a disaster, I had made it. I had cycled from Basingstoke to Benidorm. It felt somewhat surreal.

With its high-rise skyline, Benidorm, for many people, means tack, and I fully understand that it is not everyone's cup of tea. It's certainly not mine in the main. But, it is fun for a few days if you take it at face value.

With a long and rich history, the city dates life back as far as 3,000 BCE, with the Moors first creating a recognised settlement in the area in around 711 CE. They were overthrown by the Christian King, James I of Aragon and were eventually booted out in 1325, when the area was recognised as a town as a way of allowing Christians to inhabit the area.

Moving swiftly on to the last century, in 1925, and with Benidorm now well known for its fishing industry, tourism was also introduced to take advantage of the beautifully long sandy beaches and peoples' desire to sit on them.

Then, by the 1950s, with the fishing industry in decline, the local council thought they'd develop the town, aiming it solely at the tourist market.

In terms of generating a localised economy, it worked, and seventy years later, the 'New York of The Med' now attracts nearly 2.8 million visitors a year.

However, little did that council know then, that many of those visitors in modern times would be jetting out from the UK for long drunken weekends, spending wads of euros on two-for-one cocktails, tee-shirts with rude slogans, and bottle openers shaped like willies.

With the thought of nearly reaching my destination filling my head, I descended from the hills to sea level for the last time onto a long, flat coastal road leading to Altea, which seemed to be a rose between the thorns of Calpe and Benidorm. I was ahead of schedule, so decided to pop off the busy main road and down to the promenade, threading my way through the holidaymakers. It was time for my last café stop of the trip!

As I sat back, sipping my café solo, I sent a message to Lorraine asking where I should head to in Benidorm to meet. We'd planned to finish on the vast promenade that runs down the beautiful sandy beach on the northern end of the city. For all its vulgarities, Benidorm has some lovely areas, and the beach is really stunning, especially when it's empty. There was no reply.

I only had twelve kilometres to cycle, so I was starting to get a little concerned about which way to head when I got there. Still, I had about an hour or so to get that far, so I decided to carry on cycling down the sea road as far as it would let me before making my way back up onto the busy N-332 that ran towards the city.

Past L'Albir, where I would be staying that weekend in a villa, the road started to get annoyingly busy, as was my head. I felt a little frustrated as I still didn't know where to head when I got to the city, with now only six kilometres to go.

Relief from the traffic came as I eventually turned off the main road to head down into the city, past the campsites and cheap hotels on the outskirts and into the centre I recognised from previous visits.

I first visited Benidorm in 2014 to celebrate a friend's 40th birthday. There was a big group of us, and we stayed in a vast villa out of the city in a small town called La Nucia, about ten kilometres inland. The 40-year-old celebrating was the youngest person on the trip, so it wasn't exactly a weekend of clubbing, more afternoon drinking and early nights (for me, anyway).

I'd like to say it was sedate few days, except that after a very long and memorable day and evening of drinking in Benidorm on the Saturday (having just admitted I love an early night), I decided I was SAS-trained, getting back to the villa very late with the last two stragglers of the group.

We'd slid the penultimate reveller back in a taxi an hour or so earlier with strict instructions to keep the only remaining key safely in sight so that we could find it when we returned back at the secure compound. When we finally arrived back at about 1am, we couldn't find the key where we'd told him to leave it.

So, Andy McNab here decided he would climb up the wall, which I managed faster than Spiderman, before rolling over the top onto some trees on the other side to break my fall. It subsequently turned out the next day that my memory had deceived me. The trees were stick-thin spindles, like four feathers standing to attention.

Needless to say, nothing broke my fall, apart from a rock below that the top of my head said hello to very, very quickly, followed by 17-stone of drunken idiot. Luckily, and I often wonder about this, I didn't break my neck. I did, however, manage to create a gaping two-and-a-half-inch gash on the top of my head.

Slightly dazed, I managed to let the other two members of my platoon into the compound, and they sobered up as fast as you could say, 'Jesus, that looks really bad!' before we went inside the house. As luck would have it, the idiot who left before us - who shall remain nameless, Daren - had left the key hanging in the front door of the house, which he has also left wide open.

I knew the cut was bad by the worried look on my friends' faces, but went to bed anyway for a drunken sleep, which, in hindsight, was probably not the best course of action.

The following morning, I was persuaded quite quickly to go to the doctor, and my friend and I headed for a surgery. I wasn't exactly sure how healthcare worked in Spain, so I furiously phoned my bank to see how I could activate the free travel insurance I got with the account. I could finally realise some of the value from the small fortune I paid each month to have it. Unfortunately, I couldn't remember a password - amnesia perhaps, I said - so they blankly refused to help me.

The doctor in the village surgery was just as helpful. We'd gone inland rather than to the city to get help, but he looked at me like I was yet another drunken British tourist - who could blame him?

I had to have six staples punched into my head, one of which he wasn't happy with and had to pull out before powering a new one back in. Perhaps he just did it for his own amusement? No painkilling injection or pills were employed, just small pins of metal pushed straight into my head.

After he was finished, and only after he was finished, he rifled in his desk drawer and pulled out half a pack of painkillers - which turned out to be very strong - and issued me with a bill of €120.

Lesson learned, I went back again the following year, and the one after that, and luckily avoided any more injuries. Somehow, though, considering we weren't doing anything too stupid, someone in our group ended up in the hospital every single year.

Back on my bike, I'd still not received my final instructions as I approached the sea. Little did I know, lots of flapping was happening at the other end to find a suitable place for me to stop.

Finally, a quick phone call sorted my destination, and I had my orders. Google Maps was my go-to for one last time, and it duly guided me down to the promenade at the front. My first sight as I rounded the corner onto the walkway next to the glorious sandy beach – a twin mobility scooter. I'd well and truly arrived in Benidorm.

The destination ended up not being on the front at all; that would have been too simple and easy to get to. No, it was in the old town, the historic city centre.

So, I had the fun and games of cycling back off the promenade further down, then back up and through busy pedestrian areas full of families and old people wandering this way and that to buy hats, tee shirts and other knick-knacks that would be in the bin by the end of the year.

As well as people wandering around aimlessly, there were a few other cyclists as well as convoys of mobility scooters to navigate through. All thoughts of emotional endings had gone. Having enjoyed so much solitude for the past three weeks, being stuck in these crowds felt like hell.

And then, I heard the cowbells. I knew who that would be. Lorraine loves going to watch the Tour De France and has a collection of bucket hats and cowbells at home, which is not what I'd call normal. There was a huge welcome banner across the street in front of me with my face on, and inflatable clappers were in full 'slap'. As I cycled headlong into the fabric finish line, I received a massive cheer from the entire bar as passers-by stopped to see what all the commotion was.

Although I surprisingly didn't feel emotional, I was humbled that people had put in so much effort for me. I can't really say I've been that used to it in my life, which says more about my hangups than anything else and what I choose to remember, but right now, thanks in the main to Lorraine, I did indeed feel a little bit special.

My friend Matthew was there, and Gary, who had flown out with his family for a few days. Also, my good friends Rob and Jane, who had waved me off at Portsmouth, were there to greet me. The thought that people would do that for me, on top of the video I'd received the night before, well, I was somewhat overwhelmed with gratitude.

And as for Lorraine, well, she tries hard to cover it up, but she is the most loving and generous person I think I've ever met in my entire life. She also makes me feel good about myself every single day. I may have been thousands of miles from my house, but I was fully at home in her embrace.

I felt terrific. Strangers shook my hand and congratulated me, and I felt a quiet pride that I didn't feel the need to share. After all, I'm not one to gloat that I'd just cycled nearly 1,900km.

I said, I'm not one to gloat that I had just cycled 1,900km.

People looked at me for words of wisdom. I had none.

'How was it?'

'Um, good, thanks'.

'It must have been amazing?'

'Yes, it was thanks.'

It would take time to sink in, and my friends knew me well enough to gift me that space to allow that to happen. I had made so many amazing memories on my journey. But they didn't seem worth sharing just yet.

And then it was done. Things settled, the banner was put away, and I enjoyed the first of many beers that day.

50km for the day - 1,868km travelled.

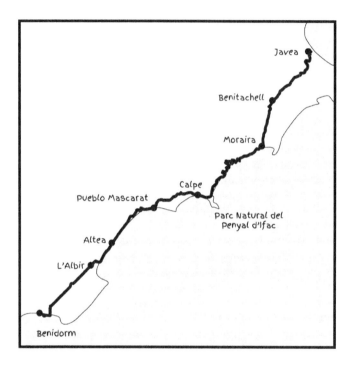

Finished

We spent a lovely weekend in Benidorm, most of which was at a quiet Villa in the hills of L'Alibir.

After arriving to a fanfare in Benidorm, and after a beer or two, we had driven Terence back to the villa in the back of the hire car, where I had a quick shower, before catching a taxi back into the city for an afternoon of chilled celebration.

With Gary enjoying a family afternoon, the rest of the group had lunch at La Cava Aragonesa, a wonderful little place in what's affectionately known as Tapas Alley, off the Place de la Constitució in the old town of Benidorm. I visited there on my fateful first trip to Benidorm, and it holds fond memories despite the eventual outcome of that particular evening.

After some cold wine and warm Tapas, we sauntered down to the front and settled in outside a bar by the beach to watch the world go by, which invariably included a few stag and hen parties well into enjoying their day.

As evening descended, we met up with Gary and his extended family, and ten of us enjoyed a large meal in a small backstreet restaurant. I felt blessed, once again, that people had put in so much effort for me as we sat chatting and eating.

The following day was all about relaxing, and it didn't feel strange - not having to pack and go - like I thought it might. Although I had been enjoying the sunshine for the past ten days, the weather back home had been awful, and my guests were lapping up the blue skies, the heat of the sun, and the cold pool. As they sat, relaxing and reading, I slowly dismantled Terence to pack him away in his travel box, talking to him like a good friend as I unscrewed nuts, removed parts and let the air out from his tyres. We'd cycled all this way and not had a single puncture!

By mid-afternoon, with people getting a bit twitchy, we made our way back into Benidorm to witness the area where the Brits go, cameras ready like a busload of Japanese tourists. I'd seen it all before, but some of the others wanted to observe it firsthand.

For reasons I still cannot fathom, one of my companions, Rob, is a very big fan of the Channel Five documentary Bargain Brits Abroad. He enjoyed regaling us with his knowledge about the campsites and dodgy-looking bars we passed, shedding some light on the lives of various characters in the show and how these locations fitted into the fabric of their lives.

Managing to park the car on a street near the 'party zone', we made our way through the small crowds to an enormous bar raised up from the street. On the balcony at the front, cheap plastic tables were grouped together, surrounded by large numbers of slouched bodies of either men or women, with stacks of empty plastic glasses in the middle.

We were smack bang in the middle of the late afternoon lull when you either go back to your room for a snooze before the evening or you just power on through. Some people had decided to split the difference and were fast asleep in their chairs.

After a pint of weak lager and some wine so sharp you wouldn't even use it for cooking, we moved onto a more upmarket bar for a drink before heading to the sticky carpets of The Red Lion, an infamous bar in Benidorm that later that night actually got raided for drugs. But by then it was starting to get a little lairy, and everyone had seen enough, so we drove back to the relative safety of L'Alibir for a slap-up meal.

The next day, our guests were gone, leaving just Lorraine and me chatting all day and enjoying the sun. We didn't even leave the villa as we tried to make our way through the overzealous shopping haul from the supermarket that would have been enough to feed a family of four for a week.

Monday soon came, and 24 days after leaving the UK, I flew back to England. It took just over two hours.

Terence travelled in the hold, and Lorraine and I enjoyed Business Class and free drinks on the short flight home to celebrate.

Epilogue

I felt in a daze for a few days when I got home. I'd been away for over three weeks, but it had felt so much longer, and it was good to be back. People asked me if I felt down or deflated. 'Why would I?' was my reply. I'd just been on the adventure of a lifetime.

Drinks were arranged for the day after I returned, and I felt overwhelmed as about twenty friends greeted me for a curry.

Eager to hear about my experience, I had nothing to offer, and I think some of them felt a little flat. In my head, I was still processing my experience. It had been so significant and life-changing, as I knew it would be, that all I could do was feebly apologise for not regaling them with any stories.

It took a good few weeks for the process to happen as I sifted through photos, videos, and notes from my trip to start writing this book. The joy of technology is that you can keep a lot of memories with just one or two small devices.

I had photos, videos, and ride data from every day, and even now, nearly five months later, I can zoom in to see street views on my computer and remember them.

I started this book by talking about my predictable life getting turned upside down and losing a lot of certainty for the future.

But, whatever the future may hold - and life continues to surprise me in good ways and bad - it's memories from journeys like this that live the longest. As I get older and the comfort of a sofa calls, I realise how important it is to keep putting myself in a position to make more of life through experiencing things I've never experienced before. And while adventures don't need to cost the earth, they offer so much more value than a new extension at home or a new car.

The amount we raised for the charity kept rising on my return, finally settling at £17,425, and I was amazed to see where that money came from, with some donations flying in out of the blue from strangers and people I had not spoken to for some while. Fundraising is hard, especially if you do it over and over, and it's crucial to find a challenge worthy of people handing over some of their hard-earned cash for a cause they are happy to donate. I am so, so grateful that they found this one worthy enough.

I wrote earlier that I believe anyone could do a challenge like this; perhaps there is a simplicity about that comment. But when people tell me how amazing it has been to watch me do my ride, or how they'd love to do something similar, there is a very, very simple answer. Go on, then.

If a 53-year-overweight me can do it, then why can't anyone? What's really stopping any of us? A friend of mine, Dave, a business coach, has a great phrase that seems to cover this very succinctly: Shit, or get off the pot.

As for me, I'm already planning another ride for a couple of years time while my legs are still able to keep turning. After all, I have new memories to make, so why wouldn't I?

Photos & Videos

You can see photos and videos of each days ride on my website, which is:

craigkillick.co.uk/benidorm24/

Acknowledgements

Although I have many thank you's to make for the support I received overall, I'd like to thank a few people personally.

Ian Fuller, our chats, your support and the things you did while I was away were amazing. But coming out to see me on the ride and that evening and day we spent together will live long into my memory, along with Cyprus and The Tourmalet. Gary Livingstone, thank you for the things you did for me. Not just the sponsorship but arranging things and coming out to see me. You have become a constant friend over many years, and I thank you for that. Rob B, thank you so much for your support in so many ways. Phenomenal as an individual, with the lovely Jane, you are unstoppable. I'd also like to thank Matthew Ripton for everything he helped me with and for coming to see me as I arrived. It was enlightening to see you away from work and relaxing.

Big thanks to my wonderful daughters, Millie, Connie, Katie and Annabelle, who afforded me the latitude to do this ride, and a special hello to my grandchildren, James and Esme, who make me feel very old and very young at the same time, and are the most inspirational teachers a 53-year-old man could have.

Finally, I'd like to dedicate this entire adventure to Lorraine. I started this book talking about getting divorced. It's a rubbish time, and we both went through it during similar periods before meeting each other. My life is so much more fun and loving with you in it. This cycling adventure was for three weeks of my life. Hopefully, our adventure will last forever.